OUR HAGGADAH

OUR HAGGADAH

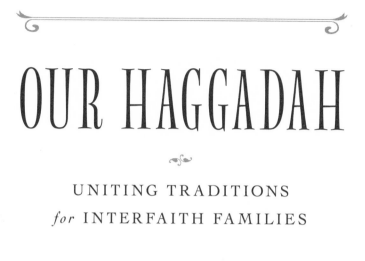

UNITING TRADITIONS
for INTERFAITH FAMILIES

COKIE & STEVE ROBERTS

HARPER
An Imprint of HarperCollins*Publishers*
www.harpercollins.com

HarperCollins books may be purchased for educational, business, or sales promotional use. For information, please write: Special Markets Department, HarperCollins Publishers, 10 East 53rd Street, New York, NY 10022.

An extension of this copyright page appears on page 139.

FIRST EDITION

Designed by Jaime Putorti
Illustrations by Kristina Applegate-Lutes

Library of Congress Cataloging-in-Publication Data

Our Haggadah : uniting traditions for interfaith families / Cokie and Steve Roberts.

p. cm.

ISBN: 978-0-06-201810-6

1. Haggadot—Texts. 2. Seder—Liturgy—Texts. 3. Judaism—Liturgy—Texts. 4. Haggadah. 5. Passover—Customs and practices. 6. Interfaith families—Religious life. 7. Passover cooking. I. Roberts, Cokie. II. Roberts, Steven V. III. Title.

BM674.643.R627 2011
296.4'5371—dc22   2010043172

11 12 13 14 15   OV/RRD   10 9 8 7 6 5 4 3 2 1

❧

To our family and friends,
who have attended our Seders for many years
and blessed Our Haggadah *with their warmth,*
their wisdom, and their wine stains

INTRODUCTIONS

❧

Did Elijah Come to Your House?
BY STEVE ROBERTS

Don't worry. We didn't have a Seder when I was growing up, either.

Yes, I was Jewish, quite Jewish, really. But for my family, Judaism was more a cultural concept than a religious one. I've run Seders for more than forty years now, yet I have no traditions or memories to draw on. My parents never taught me how to celebrate Passover because they didn't know. My grandparents didn't know, either. I taught myself (although my Catholic wife feels her constant kibitzing was an invaluable part of my education). If I can do it, you can, too.

Back in Europe, we were Jewish, because history defined us as Jews and our neighbors treated us as

Jews. That is, badly. My grandparents were all born between 1881 and 1892 in the Pale of Settlement, a vast area on the western edge of the Russian empire where Jews were allowed to live. But anti-Semitism was still deeply rooted in the local culture. My mother's father, Harry Schanbam, was a stringently secular man who would walk through the streets of his hometown of Grodno (now in western Belarus) on Saturday, the Jewish Sabbath, smoking cigarettes to show his disdain for religious rituals. Like many Jews of his time and place, politics became his religion, and as a "flaming socialist" (my uncle's description) he earned the enmity of the local Cossacks, a paramilitary force with a fondness for beating up Jews. As he used to tell me, he finally left for America after the Cossacks rode through his mother's house for the third time looking for him. My father's father, Avram Rogowsky, grew up in Bialystok (now in eastern Poland), where a vicious pogrom killed dozens of Jews in 1906. He, too, was a political radical, but his real religion was Zionism, and a year later he fled to Palestine and worked on some of the first roads built

in Tel Aviv. The dream did not last and Abe, as he came to be known in America, eventually settled in Bayonne, the town in northern New Jersey where I was born in 1943.

I knew my grandparents very well—Harry lived with us (my grandmother Sadie died before I was born), and Abe and Grandma Miriam were three blocks away. Neither grandfather had a bar mitzvah. I recall no religious symbols in their homes, no holidays, no devotions. My father and my uncles never had bar mitzvahs, and when my parents got married they followed that same secular tradition. Left-wing politics was their passion, not organized religion, and my father was at times uneasy with his ethnic background. On my birth certificate I'm Steven Rogow (the "sky" was long gone), but Dad changed it to Roberts when I was two. More American, less obviously Jewish. Growing up, I was oblivious to my sanitized name (it's Welsh, actually—lovely people, but not my people). I knew I was Jewish. Most of my neighbors and classmates were Jewish, after all. So were the local shopkeepers and my parents' friends.

We ate pastrami from Botwinick's deli, gefilte fish from Levine's market, and cheesecake from Mortman's bakery. I joined the Cub Scouts and played basketball at the Jewish Community Center. My grandfathers read Yiddish newspapers. But from Seders we knew *bupkis* (a colorful Yiddish expression meaning "absolutely nothing").

At about age twelve, I became interested in organized Judaism. My twin brother, Marc, and I actually asked our parents if we could have bar mitzvahs. I'm sure the main reason was peer pressure. All the other Jewish boys were having them, and we weren't. The presents were pretty great, too. But perhaps I was also looking for some deeper form of identity. Unlike my ancestors, I didn't feel Jewish because of history or oppression. The Cossacks (or the Nazis) were not a big threat in New Jersey. But reconnecting with organized Judaism was tricky. In Bayonne, most Jews attended the large Conservative congregation or several small shuls (Orthodox synagogues), and my parents would have felt wildly uncomfortable in any of them. A group of young professionals had recently

organized a Reform temple in town, however, and that was a better fit. So my folks reluctantly joined up and enrolled us in Hebrew school. The common story is that immigrant families stray from their Old World traditions as they become more American. In a sense I was reversing that pattern, reconnecting to my Jewish roots, to the name Rogow, which was on my birth certificate, rather than the homogenized version my father had chosen.

After my bar mitzvah I stayed active in a state-wide group called JFTY, the Jersey Federation of Temple Youth (I have a tattered old JFTY sweat-shirt framed on my wall as I write this, thanks to my aforementioned Catholic wife). Yes, I liked meeting new girls from other towns (I took Myrna Goldblatt to my senior prom), but I also enjoyed the intelligent talk about religious questions that threaded through our weekend meetings. It was my first hint of college life, of late-night bull sessions with smart people who made you think about basic issues. (One of my pals, Peter Knobel, became a rabbi, and another, Alan Kors, a history professor.) Once I got to Harvard,

most of my roommates were Jewish, as were my friends at the *Crimson*, the student newspaper, but the connections we shared were more tribal than religious. When one of my roommates got married after graduation and asked Harvard's rabbi to perform the ceremony, it was an embarrassing moment. None of us had ever met the guy.

But by then my view of religion was starting to change. I had met a girl named Cokie Boggs, a student at Wellesley, and she was an observant Roman Catholic. Cokie had attended religious schools all her life and stayed in touch with the nuns who taught her. She went to Mass regularly and one of our first dates, during spring vacation of junior year, took place in New York. We went to a movie and then stayed up all night talking. As dawn broke she went off to church, and I caught a bus back to Bayonne. My grandfather Harry was already up when I arrived home and he gave me a stern, silent look. Pop, I thought, if you only knew—I've been with a Catholic girl who's now praying in church.

Our relationship matured slowly. I was a typical

guy, petrified of commitment of any sort. More seriously, the religious issue was never far from our minds. My parents were adamantly against the match and I had always been a good son: loyal, loving, headed for a life in journalism, which they encouraged and admired. Defying them was the hardest thing I've ever done. So that meant many long talks with Cokie, many tears, many times we thought this relationship could never work. But gradually an understanding started to develop, a possible future began to take shape. We realized, eventually, that the values uniting us were far stronger than the theology dividing us. When we talked about how we wanted to live our lives, day by day, year by year—as a couple, as parents, even as grandparents—we found a common ground, a high ground, where we could build a family together. I knew it would work out when my father said to me at one point, "It would be a lot easier to oppose this marriage if it wasn't so obvious she's the perfect girl for you."

Having an understanding and working it out in practice are two different things. Mixed religious

couples can essentially choose one of three paths: they can practice no religion, pick one or the other, or do both. Different patterns work for different partners; there's no one-size-fits-all answer, but we really had only one choice. Cokie was far too observant to consider the first option. I was not nearly as devout as she was, but I was more a Rogow than a Roberts, I was on a journey that had started with my bar mitzvah years before. I could not give up my religion, and Cokie didn't want me to. In fact, part of the attraction between us was a shared devotion to our traditions, families, histories. In that sense we were both Old World and old-fashioned. So we agreed. We'd do both. We'd practice both faiths and our wedding became a test case. Instead of a church, we got married in the garden of Cokie's home (where we've now lived for more than thirty-three years). We couldn't find a rabbi to join Cokie's uncle, a Jesuit priest, in performing the actual ceremony. So we asked Arthur Goldberg, a close friend of Cokie's parents, to give a talk on Jewish teachings about marriage. We had a chuppah, a Jewish wedding canopy, and I broke a

glass, the traditional close of any Jewish ceremony. My parents and their friends felt embraced and respected. It was a good start, but only a start.

Cokie was more committed to our agreement than I was. I came to realize that if you're a person of faith, you take all religions seriously, and she shouldered the task of making Judaism a part of our lives together. I was happy to go along but she was the driving force. We now joke that she is the best Jew in the family; she replies there's never been much competition for the title. When we wrote a book some years ago about our mixed heritage, *From This Day Forward*, Cokie explained her feelings this way: "We realized that we had to create religious rituals for ourselves. Back home Steve knew that he was Jewish because it was simply part of the culture. Now, if Judaism was going to be part of our marriage, we had to deal consciously and conscientiously with the religion itself. That was particularly true for me. I couldn't make any cultural claims to Judaism, so the religious rituals became terribly important to me." She was right about that. She didn't grow up with a Yiddish-speaking grandfather or matzo ball soup (not a big loss, since she was from New Orleans and raised on shrimp rémoulade and crawfish étouffée). On our first Hanukkah together, a few months after our wedding in 1966, we happily lit the candles and left them untended when we went to bed. Bad idea. We almost burned the apartment down. But we were not deterred. The next holiday we tackled was Passover.

My mother maintained that the first Seder she ever attended was organized by her Catholic daughter-in-law. Jewish couples tend to have Seders automatically, out of custom and habit (although my twin brother married a Jewish woman and never had one). Mixed couples like us have to make a deliberate choice. And while that can be an inspiring process, it can also be intimidating. We know. We've been there. The whole point of this little book is to say, you can do it, you are not alone, here's what we've learned.

The word *haggadah* literally means "the telling" and comes directly from the biblical command to "tell your children" the story of the Jews' liberation from Egypt. The Haggadah you are now reading is essentially the same one Cokie cobbled together in 1970, and her efforts to revise and refurbish "the telling" of this story follow an ancient tradition. The first Haggadahs emerged in the period between 170 CE and 500 CE, when the rabbis of Judea started writing the Talmud, a vast collection of commentaries and analysis that still shapes Jewish law and practice. The basic Haggadah we use today was first written down by Amram bar Sheshna, or Amram Gaon, who headed a famous yeshiva in Babylon during the ninth century CE, and the first printed Haggadah was published in Soncino, Italy, in 1486. There are now more than three thousand versions, making the Haggadah "the most popular Jewish book of all time," according to Karen G. R. Roekard, editor of *The Santa Cruz Haggadah.*

So why write yet another one? For one thing, we've been approached many times by interfaith couples who are hungry for role models and rituals that reflect their lives and choices. For another, *Our Haggadah* has acquired a deep meaning for us, and our friends. It has been sanctified by years of use by the loud, loving, and occasionally sloppy crowd that attends our Seders. Each copy of the physical document has been folded and fondled, read from and spilled on by many dear friends and family members. That's the point of Passover, and we learned that very young. When I was made the *New York Times* bureau chief in Los Angeles, and we relocated to California, we left behind our entire social network. We needed to meet new people and build new connections, and most of the friends we made were from other places as well. We were all seeking the same sense of community we had left behind in North Carolina and South Dakota, Kansas City and New York City, and at our Passover Seders we forged a special bond—strangers together, perched a bit precariously on the western edge of the country, saying ancient prayers and sharing Cokie's lamb and zucchini on our mountaintop in Malibu. After five years of covering California, I was assigned to Greece, and our friends felt so keenly about the ritual that when we left for Europe, one of our going-away parties was a Seder a month early.

From the beginning our Seders, and our Haggadah, were designed to be inclusive, not exclusive. We often invited people who were like us, mixed couples, or even families with no Jewish ties. I'll always remember those wonderful ads, featuring a black boy or a Chinese man or even a befeathered Native American, with the tagline, "You Don't Have to Be Jewish to Love Levy's Jewish Rye." Well, you don't have to be Jewish to love our Seder, or any Seder. The core message of Passover—its celebration of human freedom—transcends ethnic identity. But we've sometimes had trouble adapting to new cultures. Since we arrived in Greece just before Passover, and we'd already had a Seder back in California, we decided to have a small ceremony with just our two children, Becca and Lee, who were then three and five. We were living in an apartment hotel and didn't know Athens well, but Cokie heard there was still a synagogue in an old neighborhood near the foot of the Acropolis. Go down there, she instructed, maybe a local store will be selling matzo. If you can't find any, buy pita bread, at least it's unleavened. But

I was distracted by work and neglected my assignment. I never made it to the synagogue or even the pita bakery. In a panic, as I was heading back home, I ducked into a pastry shop and bought a piece of cheesecake. Cokie was outraged. "What is this?" she demanded. "We're having a Seder with a piece of cheesecake?" "Well," I answered sheepishly, "it's Jewish." The next year we prevailed on friends who worked for the American embassy to buy matzo for us at the PX, and by the time we left Athens, the local supermarket was selling it.

In the early years we often had children's Seders to explain some of the rituals to the little ones. One of the more baffling moments comes late in the service, when a small child is asked to open the front door and look for Elijah, a prophet in ancient Israel. If Elijah shows up, the legend goes, the Messiah is on the way, and our son, Lee, was deeply disappointed when no old bearded guy appeared at our house on St. Sophie Street in the suburbs of Athens. "Daddy," he asked me, "when you were a little boy and both of your parents were Jewish, did Elijah come to your house?" Cokie reacted with amusement. "He thought Elijah was boycotting me, the shiksa" (the somewhat pejorative Yiddish word for a non-Jewish woman). Of course Elijah had not come to West 31st Street in Bayonne, either. After all, we didn't even celebrate Passover. It took Lee's shiksa mother to insist on a Seder and at least give us a shot at spotting the portentous prophet.

Moving to Greece was even more disorienting than moving to California. Every foreigner, however, was in the same boat, far from home and feeling lonely, so we made close friendships quickly. One couple that came to several Seders was Townsend and Eli Friedman. Like us, they were a Jewish-Catholic match, and their two daughters, Patricia and Elisa, were in school with our kids. One year it was Elisa's turn to look for Elijah, and she disappeared for quite a while. When she came back, we asked if she'd seen him. "No," she replied, "but I saw God." I told that story many years later at Elisa's wedding dinner. She lives in Boston now and doesn't make it down for Seder, but Patricia Friedman Bou is one of our regulars, along with her Cuban American husband, Jose, and their two daughters. It's a great joy to have several young parents, who first came to our Seders as little kids, return now with their own children.

Living in Greece not only brought us closer to the Holy Land, it brought us closer to the places in eastern Europe where my grandparents were born— and to the legacy of blood and horror those lands represented. We befriended a couple, Joe and Ulla Morris, who relocated to Athens after civil war engulfed their home in Beirut. Joe was American, a correspondent for the *Los Angeles Times*; Ulla was German, the daughter of a man who was drafted into the army during World War II and killed in France. One year Ulla asked to come to our Seder. We saw this request as a gesture of reconciliation, and to this day, it remains one of the most meaningful Passovers we've ever had. Neocosmos Tzallas, the Reuters correspondent, who had been very kind to us, came another year. Running a wire service, he was constantly concerned that news would break out, and in the age before Blackberries and cell phones he felt compelled to call his office constantly. During the Seder he never moved once, a gesture of true friendship and respect. But the instant it was over, he literally leaped for the phone.

By the time we returned to Washington and moved into Cokie's girlhood home, our Seders were a well-established ritual. The guest list started with family. From the beginning, my father and mother were so devoted that they often planned their trip north after a winter in Florida to coincide with the event. At one point Dad simply said to me, "Don't even bother to invite us, we're coming every year." My twin brother, Marc, and his kids, and younger sister, Laura, often came down from Boston. Then my younger brother, Glenn, moved to town and married an Episcopalian from New Orleans in the garden of our home; they and their girls became regulars as well. Cokie's Mom, Lindy Boggs, who served as the American ambassador to the Vatican and knows a bit about religious ritual, never misses a year. Friends were always included and we continued the tradition of inviting mainly interfaith couples.

(My parents were often among the few Jews married to each other!) There were Terry and Margaret Lenzner, who had asked me to be the godfather to their youngest child, Willy, and compensate for Terry's lack of interest in his own Jewish heritage. Emily, their oldest child, now brings her Indian American husband and small son. Mickey Kantor comes with his Protestant wife, Heidi Schulman, and accents the Hebrew portions with his soft Tennessee twang. Lesley Stahl, a Jew from Massachusetts, and her husband, Aaron Latham, a Protestant from Texas, kept coming even after they moved to New York. My college pal Joe Russin and his wife, Stephanie, returned often, even after departing for California. Millie Harmon Meyers, who attended some of our first Seders back in Malibu, often showed up with a daughter or two (she has three). Two of Cokie's dearest friends from National Public Radio also formed part of the original group: Linda Wertheimer (Protestant, New Mexico) and her husband, Fred (Jewish, Brooklyn), and Nina Totenberg (Jewish, Massachusetts) and her husband, Floyd Haskell (Protestant, Colorado). (After Floyd's death

Nina was considerate enough to marry a wonderful man and a deft Hebrew speaker, David Reines.)

Every year the guest list seemed to grow as younger couples joined the crowd and produced children. Ivan Schlager (Jewish father, Catholic mother) and Martha Verrill (Protestant father, Catholic mother) came to us for advice before their wedding, and four kids later, they're still regulars. The child of old friends, Doug Firstenberg, married Suzanne Brennan, moved in two doors away, and produced three offspring (one of them is our godchild). Two students of mine at George Washington University, Howard Opinsky (a Jew from St. Louis) and Colleen Connors (a Catholic from Connecticut), married each other, and called their two daughters my "grand students." Their younger child, Molly Rose, has for years now highlighted our Seders with her singing of the four questions. Our Jewish niece, Jenna, married her Protestant husband, Andy Mammen, in our garden, and every year they bring their two daughters down from Baltimore.

As these couples demonstrate, many young Jews are marrying outside their faith, but at the same time, they are eager to preserve and nourish their ties to Judaism. Cokie and I have long argued that organized Jewry needs to embrace these couples, not reject them, and that is clearly beginning to happen. A former student of mine was hired by several congregations on Long Island to organize programs for interfaith couples. When I spoke a few years ago at a synagogue in Louisville, the president started her annual report by emphasizing the importance of welcoming non-Jewish spouses. The Jewish Theological Seminary, which trains Conservative rabbis, has instituted seminars that teach students to deal with the reality of intermarriage. The *Jewish Week* reported that "speaker after speaker at last week's workshop urged students not to walk away but to reach out, not only to intermarried Jews and their partners, but to longtime congregants whose children have intermarried and who are fearful of being judged."

Much of Jewish life happens at home, however, not in a synagogue, and for many interfaith couples, a Seder is the perfect way to touch and taste a Jewish ritual without joining a congregation or contributing to a building fund. Cokie and I have always divided responsibilities: she inspires, organizes, and cooks for our Seders, while I preside over them, but it doesn't have to be that way. We've tried to modulate the male chauvinism built into the ritual by centuries of practice and prejudice, and in fact I have a friend, a Jewish woman married to an Irish Catholic, who writes her own Haggadah and conducts her own service every year. For anyone who takes on this task, I have a few words of advice, based on more than forty years of experience: Be not afraid. You can do it. Each Seder is the same, but also different. We all infuse the event with our own styles and personalities. Things happen and somehow they become a tradition. At our table, when the name of the Hebrew high priest Aaron is invoked, we all say it loudly because of Aaron Latham. Cokie and I have an annual fight over the order of the Exodus story, which our guests cheer on like ringside gamblers. Since I cannot sing a note, I turn the musical portion of the evening over to the NPR Songsters (Linda, Nina, Cokie, Becca). The Seder's traditional ending is, "Next year in Jerusalem," and if that phrase is meaningful to you, by all means, use it. But we don't. For many American Jews, especially those in interfaith relationships, celebrating Passover in Israel is not a deeply held desire. We say, "Next year in Bethesda." For us, it's a more honest hope that reflects our real lives.

At its center, Passover is a family celebration, so it reflects the cycles of love and loss. My dad died in 1997, and every year since I've missed his enthusiastic participation, an annual sign of his enduring gratitude to his Catholic daughter-in-law for leading the family back to its Jewish origins. My mother-in-law, the former ambassador to the Vatican, well into her nineties, still takes her turn reading. At my mother's last Seder, she was ninety-one. She died only days before I wrote this, and I already know how much I'll miss her next year. Their great-grandchildren, the twin sons of our daughter, Becca, who was three at the "cheesecake" Seder in Greece, and the daughter of our niece Jenna read portions of the service for the first time last year. We call this little book *Our*

Haggadah, but really it could be called *Your Haggadah*. You will make Passover your own holiday. You will sing your own songs, spill your own wine, say your own prayers, start your own traditions. And maybe Elijah will come to your house.

⚘

This Year in Your House

BY COKIE ROBERTS

Actually "our Haggadah" has never looked anything like this. For more than forty years, a stapled-together sheaf of papers wearing varying degrees of wine and mint sauce stains—that's been our Haggadah. The original one dates to 1970, and we still have a few copies, typed out on an old Smith-Corona, interspersed with more than a few typos, printed on that shiny paper used by the first copying machines. We revised it once, after twenty-five years, when our neighbor, and a regular participant in our Seders, Doug Firstenberg, offered to print up better-typed, more readable copies. At first, we heard howls of protest from our friends—where were the marks and mistakes? It didn't take long of course for us to infuse the "Twenty-fifth Anniversary Edition" with a new set of wine stains.

Our Haggadah has also been something of a mishmash where we go back and forth from our homemade sheets to what we call the "blue book," a Haggadah published by the Jewish Reconstructionist Foundation that we've used for decades as a supplement to the typewritten pages. Every year Steve and I argue about exactly where in the service we first move to the book, causing hoots and hollers from our longtime Seder buddies who have come to see this dispute as a Passover tradition. It's just one of the many Passover traditions—some silly, some special—that we and our friends, old and new, have come to anticipate annually as we celebrate the festival of freedom that is at the same time universal and unique. People from all countries and cultures can relate to the theme of breaking out of bondage, but it is the Jewish people who have kept alive this celebration, often risking their lives to do it, over thousands of years.

One of the most meaningful stories I've read about Passover is in Yaffa Eliach's *Hasidic Tales of the Holocaust*. She tells about a group of Jews at the Bergen-Belsen concentration camp who signed a petition asking the commandant to give them flour to bake the matzo in exchange for their daily bread ration. After they submitted the petition, when they heard nothing from their captors, the Jews were convinced that they had signed their death warrants—that they would become the sacrificial lambs. But then the word came that they could have their flour and build an oven to bake it in and they were able to produce three misshapen black matzo. They put them on a turned-over bunk bed used as a table, along with a broken pot substituting for a Seder plate. "On it there were no roasted shankbone, no egg, no haroset, no traditional greens, only a boiled potato given by a kind old German who worked in the showers." As the prisoners wept, the rabbi leading the Seder recited the Haggadah from memory. And with children surrounding him, he proclaimed the promise of Passover: "We who are witnessing the darkest night in history, the lowest moment of civilization, will also witness the great light of redemption." Even in Bergen-Belsen the rabbi insisted that his people would go from darkness to light, from slavery to freedom. That is the faith and hope that Jews all over the world and in many different languages bring to the Passover table as they ask on the same night the same question: Why is this night different from all others?

But I am not one of those Jews. I am a Catholic who feels privileged to be included in this communion. No one invited me, I pretty much wangled myself in, and that, to me, is the point of transforming our Haggadah into something a little less homespun. There are many non-Jews who want to sit at the Passover table, and many do in churches around America. That's different, however, from serving up your own Seder, which often seems intimidating at best, intrusive at worst. So this is our story of our Haggadah, and, more important, our Passover.

Even though Steve and I knew that we wanted to recognize both of our religions and rituals in our home, we had a somewhat inchoate idea of what that meant. Since Arthur Goldberg had participated in our wedding ceremony, he and Mrs. Goldberg took an interest in our marriage and very kindly invited us to their Seder in 1967, the first Passover after we were married, when we were living in New York. With some trepidation we joined in the somewhat famous Goldberg Seder, held at the time at the residence of the United States' ambassador to the United Nation, at the Waldorf-Astoria Hotel. As tuxedoed waiters served traditional dishes like matzo ball soup and gefilte fish laid out on elegant china, and the guests each took what seemed to me their very comfortable places in reading the words of the ritual, I was both mystified about what was going on and excited to be a small part of it. It wasn't until the crowd started singing freedom songs from the civil rights and labor movements, held over from the days when Goldberg had been a leading labor lawyer, that I felt I could participate with gusto.

Still, I understood that this central ceremony in the Jewish religion was one we needed to celebrate in our home. The next year, when I was pregnant with our first child, I felt even more strongly that Passover needed to be part of our fledgling adult life, but I didn't feel at all capable of doing it on my own. So I asked Steve's parents if they would host a Seder for us. They gamely said yes, though they had never held one before, and Steve's mom was not at all happy to take on the task of cooking a menu outside her usual repertoire. We went to their house in New Jersey, and the four of us read the ancient words out of the very contemporary Maxwell House coffee Haggadah. During dinner Steve's twin brother, Marc, called to talk to his folks and when their father said he would call back later because we were mid-Seder, we could all hear Marc's amazed, "WHY?" at the other end of the line. We could all also hear the whispered reply: "Because Cokie wanted it."

Well, that was certainly true. And by the next year, after we had moved to California, where we knew hardly anyone, it was clear that if "Cokie wanted it," she better figure out how to do it herself. I went in search of a Haggadah and found one in the shop of the closest temple. It was *The New Haggadah,* published for the Jewish Reconstructionist Foundation in 1942, the beloved "blue book," though now it's looking decidedly gray and missing its spine. The Haggadah did a great job of making the ceremony understandable and simple, but after the first year of using it, I found that a couple of our Jewish friends thought it omitted some parts of the service they loved, and I thought it included some preachy object lessons we could do without. So I sat down with several other Haggadahs, including of course the Maxwell House classic, plus our "blue book Bible," and wrote what has since been "our Haggadah." I changed the Twenty-fifth Anniversary Edition only by expanding gender references (the God of Abraham and Isaac became the God of Sarah and Rebecca as well, and the four sons became the four children), except where that seemed silly.

We didn't want our Haggadah to be too long—that was part of the point of writing our own—so I didn't include every prayer at every part of the service. But in picking and choosing I kept a few things in mind—first, how meaningful the particular prayers were to the Jews at the table: I had learned my first year that some recitations brought back memories that mattered a great deal; another was was whether Christians, too, might find their memories jogged by psalms they had heard during Easter services. But frankly, another consideration was keeping guests occupied while I struggled to get dinner on and off the table. As we embarked on this project of putting our Haggadah between hard covers, Steve said, "I think we should cut out 'for his mercy endureth forever.'" I was horrified. It's not only a beautiful responsorial psalm echoed joyously in the Easter Mass; it also allows me to get plates cleared and coffee served while everyone is reciting the lengthy verses. In fact there's many a year when I need the Lord's mercy to endureth a little bit longer because the cleanup takes so long.

There's so much in the Seder service that should seem familiar to someone raised in the Judeo-Christian tradition that there's no reason for first-timers to feel uncomfortable. Anyone who's been taught Bible stories as a child, much less reconsidered them as an adult, knows what Passover is about. Baby Moses in the bulrushes is one of the most common pictures decorating Sunday school classrooms, serving as a prelude to the dramatic story of the Plagues, the Exodus from Egypt, the parting of the Red Sea, and the Jewish flight to freedom. Watching the "Red Sea" part is one of the regular attractions at the Universal City theme park in California, so people who didn't learn the story in the Bible could learn it from the movies. Beyond that, Christian teaching tells us of Jesus's observance of Passover—first as a boy with his family and then as a man with his disciples, who continued to commemorate the festival in their years establishing the church.

In fact, the Passover celebration is one of the few stories told about Jesus as a child, so I remember being fascinated with it as a little girl. "Now his parents went to Jerusalem every year at the feast of Passover," Luke's gospel tells us, but when he was twelve years old, "when they had fulfilled the days, as they returned, the child Jesus tarried behind in Jerusalem; and Joseph and his mother knew not of it." I couldn't get over that. How could he stay behind without his mother knowing about it? I remember the priests trying to explain that people traveled in large family groups and that his parents probably assumed he was with cousins and other adults. It all sounded daring and fun. But then Mary and Joseph became frantic, looking for Jesus for three days until "they found him in the temple, sitting in the midst of the doctors, both hearing them, and asking them questions. And all that heard him were astonished at his understanding and answers." We are supposed to draw from the story the lesson that Jesus was learned and ready to discuss theology, that he "must be about my Father's business." But I just thought what trouble I would've gotten into if I had pulled anything like that. It also upset me on Mary's behalf—how could he worry his mother so? So it was a story I thought about a lot, and it was a story that started with the Holy Family's annual celebration of Passover.

And the most solemn week of the Christian year begins with Jesus arriving in Jerusalem to the hosannas of his followers who greeted him with palm branches as he entered the city to celebrate Passover. The gospel writers Matthew, Mark, and Luke tell us that what Christians now call the Last Supper, so often depicted in great works of art, was in fact a Seder. The Passover meal, argues the *Encyclopedia of Catholicism*, "celebrates God's liberation of the Jewish people and the continuing covenant with them. Such a celebration offers a model for understanding Christ's liberation of the world from sin through his death." It was at that meal, in his sanctification of bread and wine, that Jesus initiated the sacrament of Holy Eucharist. And some scholars believe that the wine for that first Eucharist came from the third cup of wine in the Seder, the cup of redemption, and the *afikomen* (about which more later) served as the bread. At the end of the meal, the gospels tell us, Jesus left to suffer his passion after "singing the Passover hymn." I like to think that particular Hallel, or song of praise, was the one I have insisted on—Psalm 136, that's the one where "his mercy endureth forever." Readers of the blessings in the Haggadah will hear very similar words to those in the blessings over the bread and wine in a Catholic Mass. A paper issued by the U.S. Catholic bishops reminds us that the Christian order of worship " takes its form and structure from the Jewish seder: the Liturgy of the Word, with its alternating biblical readings, doxologies, and blessings; and the liturgical form of the Eucharist, rooted in Jewish meal liturgy, with its blessings over bread and wine." The symbolism of the Easter season—the references to Jesus as the Paschal Lamb and to Christ as the Passover—those symbols make more sense once the Seder becomes familiar.

That's true about many New Testament references. When John the Baptist hails Jesus as the "Lamb of God," he's signaling that it will be Jesus, rather than the lamb, who will be sacrificed to take "away the sins of the world." It's important to keep in mind the world that the writers of the books of the New Testament were living in. Rabbi Hillel, referred to in the Haggadah, was a renowned teacher and scholar, someone whose somewhat liberal ideas certainly would have influenced Jesus and his followers. Hillel's grandson, Rabbi Gamaliel, also mentioned in the Seder service, was Saint Paul's teacher, something Paul advertised to prove his credibility as a good Jew. In the Acts of the Apostles we hear him tell a crowd in Jerusalem, "As a pupil of Gamaliel I was thoroughly trained in every part of our ancestral law." And for Paul the Passover tradition of cleaning leavening agents out of the house provides a repeated metaphor. He tells the Corinthians to "Get rid of the old leaven and then you will be a new batch of unleavened dough. Indeed you already are, because Christ our Passover lamb has been sacrificed. So we who observe the festival must not use the old leaven, the leaven of depravity and wickedness, but only the unleavened bread, which is sincerity and truth." The idea of cleaning out the "leaven" of sin before the redemptive feast finds its way into many cultures. The Greeks do their "spring cleaning" on the first Monday of Lent, called *Kathara Deftera*. The children go fly kites while the women scrub the houses and the men whitewash them in preparation for Easter. It takes a little longer—the forty days of Lent—for soul scrubbing.

Living in Greece, an ancient country so close to the Holy Land, constantly reminded us how tightly the Jewish and Christian traditions were intertwined. In fact, the Greek word *Pascha* means both Passover and Easter, and it's the most important time of the year in the Orthodox Church. One year we took the children to the Easter midnight liturgy at Saint Sophia, our local church. The entire place was pitch black until a priest lit a single candle and announced, "*Christos anesti*," "Christ is risen." Gradually, the flame was passed from hand to hand, filling the old stone structure with eerie light. Then we walked home, still carrying our burning candles, and followed the custom of making a sooty cross above our front door. It's clearly a ritual taken directly from the Exodus story, when Jews in Egypt marked their doorways with the blood of the lamb to alert God to "pass over" their houses as he carried out the most terrible of the Ten Plagues, the slaying of the firstborn.

It was on Passover that the early church celebrated

the redemption from sin that we now call Easter. It wasn't until the fourth century that the feast was moved to the first Sunday after the full moon after the vernal (sometimes called paschal) equinox. Since different traditions use different calendars, the Western and Eastern Christian churches often observe Easter on different dates. But the symbolism of going from darkness to light, from slavery to freedom, from death to life remains consistent. Look at the beautiful opening words of the Anglican Easter vigil: "On this most holy night, in which our Lord Jesus Christ passed over from death to life, the Church invites her members, dispersed throughout the world, to gather in vigil and prayer. For this is the Passover of the Lord, in which through word and sacrament we share in his victory over death."

By saying all of this I don't want you to think that I'm in any way trying to "Christianize" the Seder. Not at all. Even when Seders take place in churches, Catholic bishops discourage any attempt to "baptize" Passover, advising, "When Christians celebrate this sacred feast among themselves, the rites of the Haggadah for the Seder should be respected in all their integrity. The Seder . . . should be celebrated in a dignified manner and with sensitivity to those to whom the Seder truly belongs." And the Seder belongs to the Jewish people. I am just grateful that I am able to share in this night that is truly different from all others.

Of course my sharing in the feast also means my cooking it. And I think the thought of cooking the Passover meal is as intimidating as the recitation of the service to someone who has never done it. That wasn't as true for me as it might be for others because I had no hesitation about cooking the Seder dinner my own way. To Steve and the kids he grew up with "Jewish cooking" meant brisket and boiled chicken and delicatessen and matzo balls and gefilte fish and chopped liver. And some combination of those dishes had been part of whatever Passover meals he had attended. But to me that seemed crazy. That wasn't "Jewish" cooking (with the exception of the matzo), it was eastern European cooking, and the first Passover—thankfully, from my point of view—did not take place in eastern Europe. It took place in Egypt. And we know exactly what the main course was: lamb. Phew. I knew how to cook lamb. And from there I went on to other foods that would have been around in Egypt in the spring—eggplant, zucchini, maybe even tomatoes and okra—all much easier for me than kugel and *tsimmes*. Since Steve was not raised as an observant Jew, we do not follow the custom of cleansing our house of leaven and we don't have special china for Passover. Steve also doesn't feel the need to ask men to wear yarmulkes or skullcaps at our Seders. And though we don't regularly keep kosher, for this one night a year I am mindful of kosher rules about meat and milk and shellfish, which for a New Orleans cook isn't easy.

When I first started serving my Passover meals and insisting that I was simply taking my menu from the book of Exodus, I got a good deal of ribbing from Steve and some of our friends about my shiksa Seder. Then, happily, the *New York Times* published a piece about Sephardic Passover recipes, which looked like replicas (or instructions) for mine. The only thing on our dinner plate that is still from the European branch of the family is the *haroset*, made with apples, nuts, cinnamon, and wine (thank heaven for the food processor!) instead of the North African dried apricots, dates or raisins, and nuts. There's only so much a shiksa can insist on. And on the hors d'oeuvres table, where I put out such Middle Eastern dishes as hummus and eggplant salad with the matzo, I do include some store-bought gefilte fish and I make some chopped liver just to keep the sentimental Jews in the crowd happy.

The meal has evolved over the years as the guest list has grown. The former children at our Seders are now parents, I'm happy to say, but the burgeoning families long ago outgrew the dining room. And it's such a special night, with such a fundamental connection to Judaism, that everyone wants to keep coming year after year, which makes the celebration even more meaningful, especially to me. On other holidays with big crowds—Hanukkah and Christmas—I set up tables all over the house. But you can't do that for Passover, when everyone needs to be in the same room to participate in the service. At first we added a table to the end of the dinner table and angled it out into the hallway in an L shape. But soon that also became too small. So now we empty the glassed-in porch of all the furniture and set up rented rectangular tables. I keep saying that it looks like a VFW hall, but Steve graciously insists it really doesn't—that the warmth we intend comes through, despite the somewhat institutional-looking rows of tables. Moving all that furniture and finding a place for it can be challenging, but somehow we manage to pile pieces on top of each other and cram them into the basement. For several years I insisted that we could fit only thirty-six on the porch, and the children were exiled to another room—much to their delight. But I've decided that we can squeeze in (and I do mean squeeze) a couple of more at each table, so I've gone to forty-four. Some years that's more than enough places, if families are out of town for spring break or if some flu is raging through the elementary schools; other years, when friends bring family members or all our family shows up, it means setting up a separate kids' table in an adjoining room.

I still serve what's essentially a Middle Eastern meal (and as we go along I'll include a few recipes), though I long ago jettisoned the Greek egg-lemon, or avgolemono, soup, which was an annual favorite. It's just too hard to have soup for that many people and then clear plates and serve a main course, but I highly recommend it to a smaller group. I now have hired waiters to help with the dinner service and cleaning up, but that wasn't always the case. When we were young, there was no way we could afford such luxuries, and it took a lot of goodwill from our guests to get it all done. The main thing to keep in mind about the menu: Don't worry about it. This is a spring celebration, just go with that thought and you'll be fine. You can be sure that Jews over the centuries and around the world have served just about anything they had available.

Don't worry about any of it. This might be our Haggadah but it's your Passover—a night different from all others, filled with joy. This year in your house!

OUR HAGGADAH

THE TELLING

The telling" of the Passover story forms the core of the Seder ritual, and everything you will read about from now on—the symbols, the prayers, the practices—flows from that story. The Israelites, the tribes of Jacob, first came to Egypt to escape a famine in their own land, and Jacob's son Joseph eventually rose to a position of great power under Pharaoh, the Egyptian king. But as time went on, new kings came to fear the Israelites and made them slaves. One Pharaoh ordered the slaying of all Hebrew boy babies and

Moses's mother hid him in the reeds at the edge of the Nile to escape the edict. He was found by Pharaoh's daughter and raised in the palace, but Moses fled Egypt after killing an overseer whom he had seen abusing his fellow Jews. During his exile, God appeared to him in a burning bush and commanded him to return to Egypt and save His people. That Moses did, telling "old Pharaoh," in the words of the spiritual, to "let My people go." When Pharaoh refused, God visited nine plagues on the Egyptians, trying to force the tyrant's hand, but they did not work. Finally God decreed that all Egyptian firstborn children would be killed and he told the Israelites to smear their doorposts with blood so that He would "pass over" their houses when He carried out his decree. Pharaoh finally relented and the children of Israel fled. As they approached the Red Sea, Pharaoh had a change of heart and sent his army in pursuit, but God parted the waters, allowing the Hebrews to cross. When the Egyptians followed, the sea closed again, swallowing them up. The Israelites wandered in the wilderness for forty years before God led them to the

"Promised Land," the land of "milk and honey," west of the Jordan River. This is a story about Jews, but it is also a story about all people who live in bondage and yearn for freedom. So everyone around your Seder table—Jew and non-Jew alike—can hear the message, understand the symbols, and relate to the words that each generation is commanded to repeat.

⤞⤝

So You're Really Going to Do This

When you see pictures of a Seder table, it often looks quite beautiful but a little strange. What's that dish covered with Hebrew letters? (We'll get to that.) Do

you have to buy it? (No.) Where do you get it? (Hold on.) Do the men all have to wear yarmulkes, or skullcaps? (No.) Are special tablecloths, candlesticks, wineglasses needed? (No.) In the pictures, this night seems different because everything on the table looks different from other nights. But don't let that throw you. About the only thing you have to spend money on is matzo. Everything else can be found, made, or borrowed. (And you can even make the matzo if you want to, but you'd be nuts.)

You do need a Seder plate (that's the one with Hebrew letters) or a place to display the symbols of Passover, but that doesn't mean you have to go out and buy one. When we started our own Seders, we did choose to do that because it was easy. The same nearby temple that sold the "blue book" Haggadah also carried a good-looking Seder plate that didn't cost very much. Buying it served as a sign of commitment. As unsure as we were, we were determined to institute a Passover of our own that we would observe year after year—and we had the plate to prove it. It's traveled the world with us and suffers from one major chip, but it's still performing its duty. Over the years people have given us Seder plates, but one broke and one looks better on the children's table, if you catch our drift. Our favorite was made one year by our kids and their cousins. The cousins showed up with a big glass plate and non-toxic paint, so the children could create colorful pictures of the Passover symbols. We never should have washed that plate, or maybe we should have turned the painting into an annual event, at any rate soap and water eventually erased the precious handiwork. It's also possible to buy make-your-own Seder plate kits. (For links to these kits and many other Passover needs, see the Sources and Web Sites section at the end of this Haggadah.)

If you don't want to buy or make a special plate, you can simply put the Passover symbols (we'll get to what they mean during the service) on a big plate or tray. You need an egg (supposedly roasted but hard boiled is fine, we've even used dyed Easter eggs, so we don't waste them), a shank bone of the lamb (see, it really should be lamb for dinner, where else are you going to get a shank bone?), some parsley (or other green, such as bitter lettuce), some horseradish (we get both red and white to go on different parts of the Seder plate), and the *haroset* (recipe on page 12). You can just put little dollops of each around a plate or you could put them on little plates and then put those plates on a big tray. The thing to keep in mind is how crowded your table will get, because there are a lot of plates on the Passover table.

If you decide to buy a Seder plate, there are plenty of options. In big cities you can now find them in gift shops; your local temple or Jewish Community Center probably has a shop, and there's always the ever-helpful Internet. We do a lot of shopping from The Source for Everything Jewish, usually for fun kid stuff at Hanukkah but also for beautiful mezu-zahs as wedding and baby presents. There's both a catalog and a Web site providing a vast selection of Seder plates ranging in price from $40 to $600. (If you want men to wear yarmulkes, or *kippot*, you can buy them there, too—in every style, including ones with baseball team logos. You can also find juggling "matzo" balls and other Passover novelties.) As we sat down to write this, we also consulted Mr. Google about his choice of Seder plates, and many different styles and selections popped up.

The same is true for matzo covers. You can either buy a special cloth to contain the three pieces of matzo central to the ceremony or you can just stick them in the folds of a napkin. We've done both, but our favorite cover was made one year by two of our young regulars, Sarah and Molly Opinsky. It's tie-dyed and quite fabulous. As for the matzo itself, it's sold in regular grocery stores in many cities. If it's not locally available, Amazon.com has a wide selection of the special matzo required for Passover.

You will need a Haggadah at each place or the ability to pass one around so that everyone can join in the service. And it would be helpful, but certainly not necessary, to include on your guest list someone who can speak Hebrew, or at least recite the key parts of the service in that language. It adds a sense of continuity but also a certain solemnity to the occasion, which in our house can get fairly raucous.

For newcomers who are not Jewish, you might also give them some idea of what to expect at a Seder. One of the "kids" who grew up coming to Passover at our house failed to give her boyfriend (now husband) a heads-up the first year he came, and apparently he was somewhat startled to discover that he would be reading aloud. It's also wise to start the evening earlier than most dinner parties, since the service will take some time and it's likely to be a school night. (When Jews recall the Seders of their youth, they often describe falling asleep at the table as Uncle Artie droned on and on.) That's it for anything different, except when it comes to setting the table, which can get a little confusing.

&

The Table(s)

The Passover pictures usually show a very formal table setting, and we do tend to think of it as the "fanciest" holiday, so we dress up our VFW-type tables as best we can, with flowers and candles. Though we don't spend the days before the Seder clearing flour out of the house, we usually do try to polish the silver. But again, nothing elegant is required for the service or the celebration. Keep in mind that Jews who had nothing kept this feast alive, and it wasn't because of the quality of the tablecloths.

Observant Jews use a separate set of dishes and utensils for Passover, but since we don't keep kosher the rest of the year, we don't feel a need to follow this practice. Strict rules also say not to eat any foods (called *hametz*) made with flour and yeast—bread, cookies, pasta, cereal—during the weeklong Passover festival. Before the holiday begins, you're supposed to scour your kitchen, throwing out those products or donating them to the poor. Some families even conduct a search for crumbs on the night before the Seder, using candles or flashlights. We've never practiced this ritual, either, and it is certainly not essential; each family can decide for itself how closely it wants to follow tradition. But hunting for *hametz* can be a fun way to engage children in the holiday preparations. It's also a reminder that spring-cleaning rituals show up in many cultures. And of course there's a symbolism here: you're supposed to clean out your sins, not just your closets.

Aside from the Seder plate, which is set in front of the person leading the service, all the guests need little plates of their own with some of the special Passover food, and bowls of salt water must be accessible to everyone. Add to those the candles, wineglasses, and baskets of matzo (and in our case bottles of Tabasco), and the table gets pretty crowded. Plus you need one extra wineglass for the prophet Elijah. (Don't worry, you don't have to have food for him.)

"Elijah's cup," as it's called, can be any glass. (We found a beautiful blue one in the old ghetto in Venice years ago. It's meant to be a Kiddush cup, the wineglass for the blessing that signals the start of a significant Jewish occasion. So it seems appropriate and we love it, but it's a luxury not a necessity.) It goes in front of the leader, along with the Seder plate, the cloth containing the matzo, and a small bowl for hand washing. It's traditional also to keep a pillow nearby (we'll explain why later). When everyone sits down, each place should have a plate with horseradish, parsley, and *haroset* (we use a combination of butter plates and saucers, we don't have enough of either for our crowd). Everyone should be able to reach a bowl of salty water (we put small ones between two places) and matzo should be easily accessible to everyone (we put baskets or bowls of them on the tables). Everything else is like any regular table setting, though we knew we had hit a bad moment when we started sprinkling pairs of drugstore reading glasses around the tables and trying to find some lamps to supplement the candlelight.

～∞～

Once Your Guests Arrive

Before you sit down to the table, the evening goes like any other, except for the air of expectation that hangs over the cocktail "hour." (You hope it's not anything like an hour because that would make for an awfully late night and, no, you don't have to serve kosher wine.) Some guests may be coming in from out of town and the children have to be wrangled into their "party clothes," so there are always a few stragglers. That means we tend to sit down soon after

For the first Passover we celebrated in our own home, the only guidance for making *haroset* (this was long before the Internet, remember) came from "the blue book," which has served us so well over the years. The book describes "a mixture of grated apples, chopped nuts, cinnamon, and a little wine." That's it—no measurements, no hints on how much serves how many people. So making it was trial and error and, admittedly, a willingness to fudge a little by adding sugar. It tastes so good that in later years the kids scoffed it up, and many years later, when our daughter was living in San Francisco, she called to ask for the recipe. She had volunteered to provide the *haroset* for the Seder she had been invited to at the home of Cokie's oldest friend, another Catholic married to a Jew, in fact the son of a rabbi. We revealed the secret ingredient (sugar) and all went well. But still there was no recipe—until now. So here, for the first time, are actual measurements:

1 large apple
¼ cup chopped nuts
(meaty nuts, such as walnuts or pecans)
¼ cup red wine or less
½ teaspoon cinnamon
½ teaspoon sugar

SERVES 12

Peel and grate the apple (easiest to do the grating in a food processor).

Put the apple in a bowl and add the nuts, cinnamon, and sugar. Stir in the wine a little at a time, checking for consistency—the mixture should be moist but hold together. You might not need the full ¼ cup, depending on the size of the apple. A little *haroset* goes a long way, since you put only about a tablespoon of it on each plate. (Leftovers are good on ice cream.)

everyone has arrived. It will be a while before you actually eat dinner, so some hearty hors d'oeuvres are a good idea. Here's where we put out the gefilte fish and chopped liver, plus the Middle Eastern dips and salads. Be prepared for matzo crumbs everywhere. They're traditional! Assemble everyone at the table as soon as you think it's appropriate. If you're the cook, you'd do well to have most of the dinner ready at this point, even though you won't serve it for about a half hour. Otherwise it's hard to participate fully in the service.

Leading the Seder

By tradition Seders are usually run by men, elders of the tribe. (Steve has always conducted our Seders with Cokie feeling free to interject her strongly held views.) But gender-based distinctions like this have less meaning for many modern families and may easily be ignored. The leader should be someone who loves the ritual, understands its meaning, and can convey that to others. Being a guy, or having a *bubbe* (a Jewish grandmother) is not a requirement.

Whoever takes on the role, our advice is simple: be informal, even funny, while preserving the solemnity of the ritual. Because we have so many guests, Steve stands during the service in order to get their attention, but that's not necessary with a smaller group. People want to feel welcome and relaxed, but a Seder is not just another dinner party, either. You can start by greeting everyone, mentioning first-timers by name, perhaps recalling a few of the noteworthy things that have happened since

Writer Jim Keen, a Protestant married to a Jew, tells about being asked to lead a Seder for the first time. "My jaw dropped and nearly fell into a bowl of salt water," he writes. "It was a scary thought to me. What if I messed up? What if I sang 'Had Gadya' to the tune of 'Dayenu'? What if I didn't do it right and Moses couldn't part the Red Sea? 'Isn't there someone else more qualified?' I asked." But like many non-Jews in interfaith relationships, he got through the "scary" part and reflected afterward: "I realized that there had probably been many scenes like ours around the country. I'm not sure of the significance of this. But I do think that anything that helps make Judaism a positive experience for two young Jewish girls can't be all that bad—even if it is a Protestant dad who's trying his best."

your last time together (a bat mitzvah, a new book, a new baby). One of our favorite prayers, known as the *Shehekheyanu*, thanks God for keeping us alive and enabling us to celebrate together again this year, so it's appropriate to mark the passing of time. In traditional Seders the leader reads much of the service but we don't do it that way. We recite the major prayers together, and for the rest of the text, we ask everyone in the room to read a paragraph in turn.

This approach makes your guests feel included and respected—especially the non-Jews—and reduces the restlessness factor. Somehow, every year, a rookie gets stuck with a complicated Hebrew name. If you set the right tone, however, no one feels embarrassed if he or she mangles a word. Kids who know how to read usually like to participate, but a shy child should get a pass. We know enough Hebrew to say the main blessings, but don't worry if you don't. This Haggadah has transliterations of the Hebrew prayers that will get you through. Feeling matters more than fluency. The crowd can sometimes get unruly and that's okay. Up to a point. However, without being a drill sergeant or a Sunday school teacher, the leader

We've distilled this Seder down to a reasonable length. The portion before dinner usually takes us about forty-five minutes, perhaps a bit less. But there are always a few folks who try to speed things up and keep asking what has been called the fifth question: "When do we eat?" Some people will never be satisfied until you adopt the world's shortest Seder, which consists of these words: "They tried to kill us. We won. Let's eat."

should try hard to keep the crowd focused. The Seder tells a great story. It's worth hearing—again and again.

Before the formal ritual begins, the leader might briefly explain the main symbols of Passover, which appear on the Seder plate. Most of them will be mentioned during the service but a primer is particularly helpful to first-timers. Feel free to include your own interpretations, but here are the basics:

MATZO. Crisp, flat unleavened bread. As described in Exodus 12:39, matzo commemorates the flight of the Israelites from Egypt. They left in such haste that there was no time for their dough to rise. So while matzo symbolizes freedom and redemption, its simplicity also reminds us to be modest and humble.

MAROR. Bitter herbs, usually horseradish, sometimes mixed with beets to produce a red color. The *maror* stands for the harshness of slavery the Jews endured in Egypt. Some Seder plates, and services, call for a second form of bitter herbs, called *hazeret*; romaine lettuce (its roots have a strong, sharp taste), endive, or chicory are sometimes used. We use a different-color horseradish because our Seder plate does have spaces for both *maror* and *hazeret*, but don't worry about this one. Even the rabbis cannot agree on *hazeret*.

HAROSET. A mixture of apples, nuts, wine, and cinnamon that forms a sweet, dark paste. The word comes from the Hebrew term *kheres*, meaning "clay," and *haroset* symbolizes the bricks and mortar used by the Israelites to build the cities and storehouses of Egypt. But because *haroset* is also sweet to the taste, it expresses a hope for better days to come. The *maror* and *haroset* are eaten together during the service, combining the bitter with the sweet. Some interfaith families like to say that combining these tastes also symbolizes the blending of traditions around their table.

KARPAS. Usually a green vegetable, such as parsley or celery, but eastern European Jews sometimes use a boiled potato, because that's the only vegetable they had in the old country. The greens symbolize the coming of spring, the season  when Passover is celebrated. During the Seder they are dipped in salt water to evoke the tears shed by the Jews during slavery in Egypt.

ZEROAH. The word is Hebrew for "arm" and most Seders use a shank bone from a lamb, but a poultry bone will serve as well. The *zeroah* recalls the ancient tradition of sacrificing a lamb in the Temple in Jerusalem on the eve of Passover and then eating it at the Seder. Jews also sacrificed lambs on the night they fled Egypt; that's where they got the blood to smear on their doorposts. Vegetarians and others who dislike this symbolism can substitute a roasted beet.

The word Seder literally means "order" or "sequence" and the main elements of the ritual are pretty well established, but some Jews who feel unsatisfied by traditional practices have added their own symbols that reflect their own values. One example: putting an orange on the Seder plate as a sign of solidarity with lesbians and gay men. (An orange contains many sections and thus symbolizes the value of including everyone as part of the whole Jewish community.) Another: adding an olive to symbolize hope for Middle East peace. An increasingly popular idea is putting "Miriam's cup," filled with water, next to "Elijah's cup," to recognize the role of women in Jewish history and culture. Rabbi Geela Rayzel Raphael, writing at InterfaithFamily.com, suggests adding an artichoke to the Seder plate at an interfaith service and explains: "Like the artichoke, which has thistles protecting its heart, the Jewish people have been thorny about this question of interfaith marriage. Let this artichoke on the Seder plate tonight stand for the wisdom of God's creation in making the Jewish people a population able to absorb many elements and cultures throughout the centuries—yet still remain Jewish."

BEITZAH. A cooked egg, sometimes baked or roasted. It does not play a direct role in the service but it has many meanings. Above all, it symbolizes spring and new life. But eggs are also part

of the traditional Jewish mourn-
ing ritual, the first meal served
to Orthodox families after they
bury a loved one. So the *beitzah*
is said to recall the destruction of
the Temple in Jerusalem in 70 CE.

Before the official "order" of the Seder begins,
many families like to light candles, a familiar part
of many Jewish rituals. Usually it is the mother of
the family, or other female relatives, who light the
candles. This can be done at sundown, before your
guests arrive, or when they first sit down. Here is the
first blessing:

בָּרוּךְ אַתָּה יהוה אֱלֹהֵנוּ מֶלֶךְ הָעוֹלָם אֲשֶׁר קִדְּשָׁנוּ בְּמִצְוֹתָיו וְצִוָּנוּ לְהַדְלִיק
נֵר שֶׁל [שַׁבָּת וְשֶׁל] יוֹם טוֹב.

Barukh atah Adonai eloheinu melekh ha-olam,
Asher kid'shanu be-mitzvotav ve-tzivanu
Le-hadlik ner shel [Shabbat ve-shel] yom tov.

Blessed be thou O Lord our God, Ruler of the
Universe

*Who has commanded us to light the [Sabbath and]
holiday candles.*

Some families add a second prayer, which is repeated in the actual service itself.

בָּרוּךְ אַתָּה יהוה אֱלֹהֵנוּ מֶלֶךְ הָעוֹלָם שֶׁהֶחֱיָנוּ וְקִיְּמָנוּ והגיעָנוּ לַזְמַן הַזֶּה.

*Barukh atah Adonai eloheinu melekh ha-olam,
She-hekh-eyanu ve-ki'y'manu ve-higiyanu la-z'man
ha-zeh*

*Blessed be Thou, O Lord our God, Ruler of the
Universe, who has kept us in life, sustained us,
and allowed us to reach this season.*

One ritual you may want to follow at this point: asking each guest to say a silent prayer or wish to start the celebration.

Now the formal Seder begins.

THE FIRST CUP OF WINE: SANCTIFICATION

(Some Haggadahs say the wineglasses should be filled at this point. With a large crowd that likes to drink, we prefer to fill them before people sit down at the table.)

LEADER: We drink four cups of wine during the Seder. Now we say a prayer of thanksgiving together before drinking the first cup. Those of you who know the Hebrew, please join in.

Kiddush

בָּרוּךְ אַתָּה יהוה אֱלֹהֵנוּ מֶלֶךְ הָעוֹלָם בּוֹרֵא פְּרִי הַגָּפֶן.

Barukh atah Adonai eloheinu melekh ha-olam,

borei p'ri ha-gafen.

Blessed be Thou, O Lord our God, Ruler of the

Universe, who creates the fruit of the vine.

בָּרוּךְ אַתָּה יהוה אֱלֹהֵנוּ מֶלֶךְ הָעוֹלָם אֲשֶׁר בָּחַר בָּנוּ מִכָּל־עָם וְרוֹמְמָנוּ
מִכָּל־לָשׁוֹן וְקִדְּשָׁנוּ בְּמִצְוֹתָיו. וַתִּתֶּן לָנוּ יהוה אֱלֹהֵנוּ בְּאַהֲבָה [שַׁבָּתוֹת
לִמְנוּחָה וּ] מוֹעֲדִים לְשִׂמְחָה חַגִּים וּזְמַנִּים לְשָׂשׂוֹן אֶת יוֹם [הַשַּׁבָּת הַזֶּה,
וְאֶת־יוֹם] חַג הַמַּצּוֹת הַזֶּה זְמַן חֵרוּתֵינוּ [בְּאַהֲבָה] מִקְרָא קֹדֶשׁ זֵכֶר לִיצִיאַת
מִצְרָיִם. כִּי בָנוּ בָחַרְתָּ וְאוֹתָנוּ קִדַּשְׁתָּ מִכָּל־הָעַמִּים [וְשַׁבָּת] וּמוֹעֲדֵי קָדְשֶׁךָ
[בְּאַהֲבָה וּבְרָצוֹן] בְּשִׂמְחָה וּבְשָׂשׂוֹן הִנְחַלְתָּנוּ. בָּרוּךְ אַתָּה יהוה מְקַדֵּשׁ
[הַשַּׁבָּת וְ] יִשְׂרָאֵל וְהַזְּמַנִּים.

The number four recurs throughout the Seder: four cups of
wine, four questions, four kinds of children, four loud uncles
(the last one is a joke). There are many explanations in rab-
binic tradition for why we drink four cups of wine at the Seder.
The most common is that God promised to free the Israelites
four different times before the Exodus occurred. Some commentators have given each cup its own name: Sanctification,
Deliverance, Redemption, and Restoration. Others (Surprise!
An argument!) name the cups after the four matriarchs: Sarah,

Rebecca, Rachel, and Leah. However, we do not limit wine consumption at our Seder to four cups, and we put bottles of wine on the tables so that people may help themselves.

Barukh atah Adonai eloheinu melekh ha-olam,
asher bakhar banu mi-kol am ve-rom'manu
mi-kol lashon ve-kid'shanu be-mitzvotav.
Va-titen lanu, Adonai eloheinu, be-ahavah
[Shabbatot li-m'nuchah u-] mo'adim le-simchah,
khagim u-z'manim le-sasson, et yom [ha-
Shabbat ha-zeh ve-et yom] Khag ha-Matzot
ha-zeh, z'man kheruteinu [be-ahavah] mikra
kodesh, zekher litziyat Mitzrayim. Ki vanu
vakharta ve-otanu kidashta mi-kol ha-amim,
[ve Shabbat] u-mo'adei kodsh'kha [be-ahavah
u-v'ratzon] be-simkhah u-v'sasson hinkhaltanu.
Barukh atah Adonai, mekadesh [ha-Shabbat
ve-] Yisrael ve-ha-z'manim.

Blessed be Thou, O Lord our God, Ruler of the
Universe, who has chosen us among all nations

*and sanctified us by thy commandments. You
have given us festivals for rejoicing [Sabbath
and], this feast of unleavened bread, the time
of our liberation from bondage in Egypt. You
selected us to inherit the [Sabbath and] holy
feast days. Praised be Thou, O Lord, who hallows
Israel and the festivals.*

בָּרוּךְ אַתָּה יהוה אֱלֹהֵנוּ מֶלֶךְ הָעוֹלָם שֶׁהֶחֱיָנוּ וְקִיְּמָנוּ והגִיעָנוּ לַזְמַן הַזֶּה.

*Barukh atah Adonai eloheinu melekh ha-olam,
She-hekh-eyanu ve-ki'y'manu ve-higiyanu la-z'man
ha-zeh.*

*Blessed be Thou, O Lord our God, King of the
Universe, who has kept us in life, sustained us
and allowed us to reach this season.*

(Drink the first cup of wine.)

WASHING THE HANDS

LEADER: According to custom, we wash our hands as a sign that we are purified and prepared to participate in the Seder, but we say no blessing.

(At our Seders Steve dips his hands in the bowl provided. Other families pass around pitchers, bowls, and towels for everyone to wash hands, but that's harder with larger crowds and not necessary.)

DIPPING THE GREENS

(We all take our parsley and dip it in the bowls of salt water.)

The word *karpas* means "greens" in Hebrew, but in Greek it means "appetizer." At this point in the Seder, guests are sometimes encouraged to follow an ancient custom: snacking on vegetables and dips placed on the table. This is particularly useful at more traditional services that take a while before getting to dinner.

LEADER: These greens are a symbol of the coming of spring. Before partaking of them let us say together:

בָּרוּךְ אַתָּה יהוה אֱלֹהֵנוּ מֶלֶךְ הָעוֹלָם בּוֹרֵא פְּרִי הָאֲדָמָה.

Barukh atah Adonai eloheinu melekh ha-olam,
   borei p'ri ha-adamah.

Blessed be thou, O Lord our God, Ruler of the
   Universe, who creates the fruit of the earth.

BREAKING THE MATZO

**(The leader uncovers the three pieces of matzo,
breaks the middle piece, leaves half on the plate,
and holds up the other half. The leader, or another
guest, then says:)**

Behold the matzo, the bread of affliction our ancestors ate when they were slaves in Egypt. Let all who
are hungry and in distress come and celebrate with
us. Would that all who are in need could join our
Pesach feast.

(Someone—it's often a teenager in our house—then takes that broken piece of matzo, called the *afikomen*, and hides it.)

The *afikomen* is a reminder that others are less fortunate than we are and sometimes go hungry. The obligation of *tzedakah*—meaning charity or righteousness—is central to Judaism, and some families mark Passover by making a contribution to a food bank or soup kitchen. Others suggest that Seder guests contribute small sums toward a joint donation. After dinner, the younger children are allowed to hunt for the *afikomen*, and the competition can get pretty fierce. We limit the possible hiding places to the first floor—behind cushions and inside drawers are favorites—so that the mayhem is contained. And we give the winner a small prize, like Magic Markers or Passover candy. We've had parents suggest that all children are "winners" and should get prizes but we don't listen to them.

THE FOUR QUESTIONS

(These are traditionally asked, or sung, by the youngest child who can read or recite. We usually divide them among four children so that more can participate in this central moment of the Seder. If no children are present, adults can read them. It's nice to hear them said in Hebrew but English is fine, too.)

מַה נִשְׁתַּנָּה הַלַּיְלָה הַזֶּה מִכָּל־הַלֵּילוֹת? שֶׁבְּכָל. הַלֵּילוֹת אָנוּ אוֹכְלִין חָמֵץ
וּמַצָּה. הַלַּיְלָה הַזֶּה כֻּלּוֹ מַצָּה.

Mah nishtanah ha-lailah ha-zeh mi-kol ha-leilot?

She-be-khol ha-leilot anu okhlin hametz u-matzah,

ha-lailah ha-zeh kulo matzah?

Why is this night different from all other nights?

On all other nights we eat either leavened or

unleavened bread, why on this night do we eat

only unleavened bread?

שֶׁבְּכָל הַלֵּילוֹת אָנוּ אוֹכְלִין שְׁאָר יְרָקוֹת הַלַּיְלָה הַזֶּה מָרוֹר.

She-be-khol ha-leilot anu okhlin she'ar yerakot, ha-

lailah ha-zeh maror?

On all other nights we eat herbs of all kinds, why on

this night do we eat bitter herbs?

שֶׁבְּכָל הַלֵּילוֹת אֵין אָנוּ מַטְבִּילִין אֲפִלּוּ פַּעַם אֶחָת הַלַּיְלָה הַזֶּה שְׁתֵּי פְעָמִים.

She-be-khol ha-leilot ein anu matbilin afilu pa'am

ekhat, ha-lailah ha-zeh sh'tei fe'amim?

On all other nights we never dip herbs in water, why on this night do we dip herbs twice?

שֶׁבְּכָל הַלֵּילוֹת אָנוּ אוֹכְלִין בֵּין יוֹשְׁבִין וּבֵין מְסֻבִּין וּבֵין מְסֻבִּין הַלַּיְלָה הַזֶּה כֻּלָּנוּ מְסֻבִּין.

She-be-khol ha-leilot anu okhlin bein yoshvin u-vein mesubin, ha-lailah ha-zeh kulanu mesubin?

On all other nights we eat sitting at the table, why on this night do we all recline at the table?

The "reclining" part is an odd custom and a bit hard to duplicate, especially if your table is as crowded as ours. One option: everyone can sort of lean in unison to simulate reclining. Or you can provide the guests small pillows to place behind their backs. The Obamas did this when they hosted a Seder at the White House, but again, this is a custom better suited to a small crowd (or a large supply of government-issue pillows). It's easier to have the leader act out the symbolic gesture for everyone (having a pillow available adds to the meaning but is not essential).

ANSWERS TO THE FOUR QUESTIONS

Why do we eat only unleavened bread? When the Jews left Egypt it was in great haste. The dough had no time to rise.

Why do we eat bitter herbs? Because the lives of the Jews in Egypt were bitter with hard labor.

Why do we dip the herbs twice? We dip the greens in salt water as a symbol of rebirth, the bitter herbs in the *haroset* because the despair of slavery was sweetened by the promise of freedom.

Why do we recline? Reclining at the table was the sign of a free person—so we commemorate the freedom of Passover.

The core meaning of the Seder is to teach the liberation story to your children. In Exodus 13:3 Moses says to the Israelites, "Remember this day, the day on which you have come out of Egypt," and adds, "On that day you are to tell your son, 'This is because of what the Lord did for me when I went forth from Egypt.'" Fortunately, we are well past the notion that only sons should ask the questions or learn the answers taught at Passover. Many old customs are worth keeping, but this is not one of them.

THE STORY OF THE EXODUS: THE FOUR CHILDREN

Once we were slaves of Pharaoh in Egypt, but the Lord our God brought us forth with a strong hand and an outstretched arm. If God had not brought our forebears out of Egypt, then we and our children and our children's children might still be enslaved. Therefore, even if we were all wise, even if we all had understanding and were learned in the Torah, it would still be our duty to tell and retell the story of the Exodus. The more we dwell upon the story of the Exodus, the deeper will be our understanding of what freedom means and the stronger our determination to win it for ourselves and for others.

The story is told of Rabbi Eliezer, Rabbi Joshua, Rabbi Eleazar ben Azariah, Rabbi Akiba, and Rabbi Tarfon recounting the story of the Exodus all night until their students came to them in the morning and said it is time to recite the Shema (*sh-MAH*).

So the story of the Exodus is told to children throughout the ages. But all children are not alike

The Shema is the most important prayer in Judaism and is said twice daily by observant worshippers: "Hear, O Israel: the Lord is our God, the Lord is one." Rabbi Tarfon's odd-sounding name (he could be a character from *Star Wars* or a Japanese car) has always been something of a joke in our family, so we looked him up. He lived in the first century CE and is described as both very wealthy and quite modest. His teaching stressed the importance of improving the world even when the task seems hopeless. One quote attributed to Rabbi Tarfon: "The day is short, the task is great, the laborers are lazy, the reward is great, and the Master [i.e., God] of the house is insistent."

and they must be told in different ways. According to the rabbis, there are four types of children.

The first is the wise child. She loves Pesach, she is eager to celebrate the holiday and asks, "What are the decrees, statutes, and laws that the Lord our God has commanded concerning Passover?" She must be told all the laws of the festival because they symbolize freedom for all. (And she must be told after the Paschal lamb, no dessert.)

Then there is the wicked child. He asks, "What does this service mean to *you*?" By phrasing it this

We have always included this phrase about "no dessert," but were never quite clear what it meant. One interpretation: in ancient tradition the Paschal lamb was always the last dish served at the Seder. Another version: the *afikomen* becomes a symbol for the Paschal lamb, so once it is found and consumed after dinner, no other dishes should be eaten. A third version: the *afikomen* (both as a piece of matzo and as a symbol for the lamb) should be the last taste in your mouth at the end of the Seder. Pick your own version, but in essence the phrase means that children should be taught the rules and traditions.

way, he excludes himself from the question and cuts his ties to the community. It is therefore proper to answer him saying, "This is because of what the Lord did for *me* when *I* went forth from Egypt," implying that if he had been there, he would not have been worthy of redemption. The point is to help this child see a personal connection to the Passover story.

The simple child asks, "What is this all about?" To her you provide a direct answer: "With a strong hand, the Lord brought us forth from Egypt, from the house of bondage."

The fourth kind of child is the one who lacks the capacity to inquire at all. To him you simply say, as the Torah says, "This is because of what the Eternal did for me when *I* went forth from Egypt."

The story of the four children is necessary because the Torah includes four different versions of the command that the parents tell the story of the Exodus to their children. So the rabbis, struggling to comply with the Torah's dictates, devised a different type of child for each version of the story.

THE NARRATIVE

(The retelling of the actual Exodus story is not in some Haggadahs but we have found it useful over the years. We follow the maxim: you cannot tell a good story too many times. This version is condensed from the Revised English Bible.)

When there was famine in Canaan, "Jacob and all his family with him, his sons and their sons, his daughters and his sons' daughters, he brought them all to Egypt." Jacob's son Joseph was the prime

minister to the Pharaoh, who welcomed into his land
Jacob and all of his family.

This is the point in the service where we've had our annual fight.
We never wrote down the narrative in one place, but read it from
the "blue book," passing our increasingly tattered copy among
our guests and skipping portions to shorten the time. But we
never agreed on what should be included or omitted. The inevi-
table result: our guests got confused and we got testy. So we've
finally done what we should have done years ago: agreed on a
text that confuses no one. Our regular crowd might mourn the
loss of a long-running tradition, but we won't.

"In the course of time, Joseph and all his
brothers and that entire generation died. The
Israelites were prolific and increased greatly, be-
coming so numerous and strong that the land was
full of them. When a new king ascended the throne
of Egypt, one who did not know Joseph, he said
to his people, 'These Israelites have become too
many and too strong for us. We must take steps to
ensure that they increase no further; otherwise we
shall find that, if war comes, they will side with the

enemy, fight against us, and become masters of the country.'

"So taskmasters were appointed over them to oppress them with forced labor. This is how Pharaoh's store cities, Pithom and Ramses, were built. But the more oppressive the treatment of the Israelites, the more they increased and spread, until the Egyptians came to loathe them. They ground down their Israelite slaves, and made life bitter for them with their harsh demands, setting them to make mortar and bricks and to do all sorts of tasks in the fields.

"Pharaoh then issued an order to all the Egyptians that every newborn Hebrew boy was to be thrown into the Nile, but all the girls were to be allowed to live."

A Levite woman "conceived and bore a son, and when she saw what a fine child he was, she kept him hidden for three months. Unable to conceal him any longer, she got a rush basket for him, made it watertight with pitch and tar, laid him in it, and placed it among the reeds by the bank of the Nile. The child's

sister stood some distance away to see what would happen to him.

"Pharaoh's daughter came down to bathe in the river, while her ladies-in-waiting walked on the bank. She noticed the basket among the reeds and sent her slave girl to bring it. When she opened it, there was the baby; it was crying and she was moved with pity for it. 'This must be one of the Hebrew children,' she said. At this the sister approached Pharaoh's daughter: 'Shall I go and fetch you one of the Hebrew women to act as a wet nurse for the child?'"

The baby was taken to his mother who nursed him and raised him. "Then, when he was old enough, she brought him to Pharaoh's daughter, who adopted him and called him Moses, 'because,' said she, 'I drew him out of the water.'

"One day after Moses was grown up, he went out to his own kinsmen and observed their labors. When he saw an Egyptian strike one of his fellow Hebrews he looked this way and that and, seeing no one about, he struck the Egyptian down and hid his body in the sand.

"When it came to Pharaoh's ears, he tried to have Moses put to death, but Moses fled from his presence and went and settled in Midian." There he married the daughter of Jethro and became the shepherd of Jethro's flock.

"Years passed, during which time the king of Egypt died, but the Israelites still groaned in slavery. They cried out and their plea for rescue ascended to God." One day when Moses was tending the sheep of his father-in-law he saw "a fire blazing out from a bush. Although the bush was on fire, it was not

Moses's time in Midian has an important implication for the Seder. He first met his wife, Zipporah, when she and her sisters were drawing water from a well. The young women were harassed by a band of shepherds and Moses chased the troublemakers away. When Zipporah told her father about the incident he said of Moses, "Then where is he? Why did you leave him there? Go and invite him to eat with us." The young couple named their first child Gershom, which means, "a sojourner there," and Moses explained the choice by saying, "I have been a stranger in a strange land." The incident helps explain why strangers, or newcomers, are traditionally welcome at Seders. It also explains one of the most solemn of all Jewish commandments: "Eat something!" By the way, Zipporah was not a Hebrew, and has often been depicted as a strong woman of color. That's about as mixed a marriage as you can get.

being burnt up, and Moses said to himself, 'I must go across and see this remarkable sight. Why ever does the bush not burn away?' When the Lord saw that Moses had turned aside to look, he called to him out of the bush, 'Moses, Moses!' He answered, 'Here I am.'

"The Lord said, 'I have witnessed the misery of my people in Egypt and have heard them crying out because of their oppressors. I know what they are

suffering and have come down to rescue them from the power of the Egyptians and to bring them up out of that country into a fine, broad land, a land flowing with milk and honey.

"'Come, I shall send you to Pharaoh, and you are to bring my people out of Egypt.' 'But who am I,' Moses said to God, 'that I should approach Pharaoh and that I should bring the Israelites out of Egypt?' God answered, 'I am with you.'" God told Moses to appoint his brother, Aaron, as his spokesman "and he will tell Pharaoh to let the Israelites leave his country. But I shall make him stubborn, and though I show sign after sign and portent after portent in the land of Egypt, Pharaoh will not listen to you."

The Pharaoh refused to allow the people of Israel to leave Egypt, so the Lord sent plague after plague on Pharaoh and the Egyptians. Nine plagues the Lord inflicted on the Egyptians but still Pharaoh remained stubborn until God sent the tenth plague—the killing of the firstborn. But first, God instructed Moses to tell the Israelites to slay a lamb and "take

some of the blood and smear it on the two doorposts and on the lintel of the house.

"It is the Lord's Passover. On that night I shall pass through the land of Egypt and kill every first-born of man and beast. Thus I shall execute judgment, I the Lord, against all the gods of Egypt. As for you, the blood will be a sign on the houses in which you are: when I see the blood I shall pass over you; when I strike Egypt, the mortal blow will not touch you. You are to keep this day as a day of re-membrance, and make it a pilgrim-feast, a festival of the Lord; generation after generation you are to ob-serve it as a statute for all time."

And so with the terrible tenth plague, "Pharaoh summoned Moses and Aaron while it was still night and said, 'Up with you! Be off, and leave my people, you and the Israelites. Go and worship the Lord, as you request.'

"And on that very day the Lord brought the Is-raelites out of Egypt.

"Then Moses said to the people, 'Remember this day, the day on which you have come out of Egypt, the land of slavery, because the Lord by the strength of his hand has brought you out.'

"When it was reported to the Egyptian king that the Israelites had gone, he and his courtiers had a change of heart.

"The Egyptians, all Pharaoh's chariots and horses, cavalry and infantry, went in pursuit, and overtook them encamped beside the sea. The Lord said to Moses, 'You are to raise high your staff and

hold your hand out over the sea to divide it asunder, so the Israelites can pass through the sea on dry ground.'

"And the Israelites went through the sea on dry ground, while the waters formed a wall to the right and left of them.

"Then the Lord said to Moses, 'Hold your hand out over the sea, so that the water may flow back on the Egyptians, their chariots and horsemen.' Moses held out his hand over the sea, and at daybreak the water returned to its usual place and the Egyptians fled before its advance, but the Lord swept them into the sea. As the water came back it covered all Pharaoh's army, the chariots and cavalry, which had pressed the pursuit into the sea. Not one survived.

"That day the Lord saved Israel from the power of Egypt."

THE TEN PLAGUES

These are the plagues the Lord unleashed upon the Egyptians:

(As the plagues are read, the leader dips a finger in a wineglass and then drips a drop on a plate for each affliction. Traditionally the wine was dripped on the tablecloth but the plate avoids stains.)

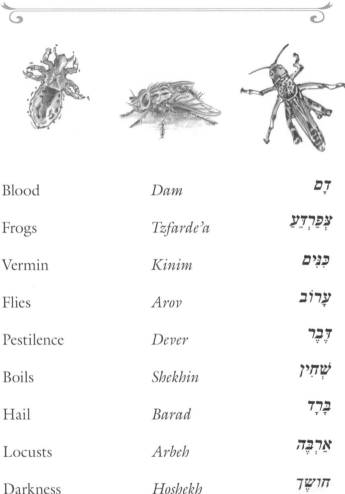

Blood	*Dam*	דָּם
Frogs	*Tzfarde'a*	צְפַרְדֵּעַ
Vermin	*Kinim*	כִּנִּים
Flies	*Arov*	עָרוֹב
Pestilence	*Dever*	דֶּבֶר
Boils	*Shekhin*	שְׁחִין
Hail	*Barad*	בָּרָד
Locusts	*Arbeh*	אַרְבֶּה
Darkness	*Hoshekh*	חוֹשֶׁךְ

Slaying of the Firstborn *Makkat Bekhorot* מַכַּת בְּכוֹרוֹת

The recitation of the Ten Plagues provides a good opportunity to involve children in the Seder. One year, Steve's sister Laura sent us masks depicting the plagues. We hand out the masks to ten little ones, and when their "plague" is read, they jump up with the mask on. If you don't have ten kids, obviously they can double up on the plagues. As an alternative to masks, Ten Plagues finger puppets are widely available. The Web site Chai Kids sells Ten Plagues in a Box, ten small toys each representing a different affliction; or you can get a bag of plastic frogs that kids can throw at each other during the reading of the second plague. (You can also buy a batch of Ping-Pong balls at a sporting-goods store and simulate hail.) Chai Kids also offers a wide array of Passover gift ideas: from an inflatable matzo ball to a Pharaoh punching bag and a burning bush hand puppet. Another option is having kids make their own Passover crafts. Aish.com contains suggestions for acting out the Ten Plagues, although they say about the slaying of the firstborn, "Don't try this one at home." Substitute the parting of the Red Sea as an option. Good call.

DAYENU

(*Dayenu* means "it would have been sufficient" or
"that would have been enough." This is a traditional
song of thanksgiving, sung after the telling of the
Exodus story. We recite it together in English; then
those who know it in Hebrew sing a few verses.)

How many wonderful deeds did God perform
   for us!
Had he brought us out of Egypt and not split
   the Red Sea, *dayenu.*

Had he split the sea and not brought us through on dry land, *dayenu*.

Had he brought us through on dry land and not drowned the oppressors in the sea, *dayenu*.

Had he drowned our oppressors and not sustained us in the wilderness for forty years, *dayenu*.

Had he sustained us in the wilderness for forty years and not fed us manna, *dayenu*.

Had he fed us manna and not given us the Sabbath, *dayenu*.

Had he given us the Sabbath and not brought us to Mount Sinai, *dayenu*.

Had he brought us to Mount Sinai and not given us the Torah, *dayenu*.

Had he given us the Torah and not led us into the land of Israel, *dayenu*.

Had he led us into Israel and not built the Temple, *dayenu*.

How much more then are we to be grateful to God for the wonderful deeds he performed for us. He brought us out of Egypt and split the Red Sea for us and brought us through on dry land and drowned our oppressors and sustained us in the wilderness for forty years and fed us with manna and gave us the Sabbath and brought us to Mount Sinai and gave us the Torah and led us into the land of Israel and built the temple!

In its entirety, "Dayenu" is fifteen verses long. Even diehards don't usually sing the whole thing. Here are the first three verses transliterated from the Hebrew, enough for most gatherings. For those who don't know the tune, many Web sites, such as The Holiday Spot, have recordings that can give you a sense of the melody. The sheet music is available at musicnotes.com.

Ilu ho-tsi, ho-tsi-a-nu,   Had He brought all,
Ho-tsi-a-nu   brought all of us,
    mi-Mitz-ra-yim,   brought all of us out
Ho-tsi-a-nu   from Egypt,
    mi-Mitz-ra-yim,   then it would have been
Da-ye-nu!   enough. Oh, dayenu.

CHORUS:

Dai, da-ye-nu,
Dai, da-ye-nu,
Dai, da-ye-nu,
Da-ye-nu, da-ye-nu, da-ye-nu!

Dai, da-ye-nu,
Dai, da-ye-nu,
Dai, da-ye-nu,
Da-ye-nu, da-ye-nu!

Ilu na-tan, na-tan la-nu,   Had He given, given to us,
Na-tan la-nu et-ha-Sha-bat, given to us all the
Na-tan la-nu   Sabbath,
    et-ha-Sha-bat,   then it would have been
Da-ye-nu!   enough. Oh, dayenu.

CHORUS

Ilu na-tan, na-tan la-nu, Had He given, given to us,
Na-tan la-nu et-ha-To-rah, given to us all the Torah,
Na-tan la-nu et-ha-To-rah, then it would have been
Da-ye-nu! enough. Oh, dayenu.

CHORUS

THE SYMBOLS OF PESACH

Rabbi Gamaliel said that whoever does not explain the three most important symbols of Pesach has not truly celebrated the feast.

When our Haggadah was reprinted for the twenty-fifth-anniversary edition, we missed one typographical error: it says "Rabbit Gamaliel." That's how traditions get started. We've always giggled at the thought of an aged bunny in a skullcap issuing talmudic edicts. So we'll miss that old rabbit.

(The leader raises the shank bone, but we usually have guests read the explanations.)

This bone symbolizes the Paschal Lamb. After many years of wandering in the desert, the Israelites came to dwell in their own land, and families would bring a lamb to the Temple in Jerusalem as a Passover offering. As the Torah tells us, it is a reminder that "God passed over the houses of the Israelites in Egypt when he smote the Egyptians and spared our houses."

(The leader raises the matzo.)

The meaning of the matzo is threefold. First, it is a symbol of the poverty and enslavement endured by our ancestors in Egypt, and should inspire us to work for peace and justice for all people in our day. Second, because our ancestors had to flee Egypt in haste, there was no time for the bread to rise. As the Torah tells us, "They baked unleavened cakes of the dough which they had brought forth out of Egypt." Third, the matzo represents a time when our ancestors lived simply and should remind us that acts of kindness and charity are more important than material luxuries.

(The leader points to the *maror*, or bitter herbs.)

Why do we eat the *maror*? Because the Egyptians embittered the lives of our ancestors. As the Torah tells us, "They made their lives bitter with hard labor in mortar and brick and in all manner of labor in the field, all their service was imposed on them with rigor."

There are many references to the Torah in this service, and the phrase might not be familiar to non-Jews. The word means "teaching" or "law" in Hebrew and refers to the first five books of the Old Testament: Genesis, Exodus, Leviticus, Numbers, and Deuteronomy. According to Jewish tradition, they were divinely inspired and revealed to Moses on Mount Sinai in 1312 BCE, so they are sometimes called the Five Books of Moses, or the Pentateuch. In Jewish ritual, the books are hand-inscribed on parchment scrolls and stored in a special place in the synagogue, called the ark. A different portion is read during each Sabbath service throughout the year. Of course the Torah, as part of the Old Testament, is holy to Christians as well.

THE SECOND CUP OF WINE: DELIVERANCE

(Fill the second cup of wine. You can say
this portion together or have guests read the
paragraphs separately.)

In every generation we should all feel as though
we each took part in the Exodus from Egypt. As the
Torah tells us, "and thou shalt tell thy son on that
day saying, 'This is because of what the Lord did for
me when *I* went forth from of Egypt." In this generation, too, we should feel as though we ourselves
were freed when the Israelites left Egypt.

(Raise the wineglass.)

We should therefore thank, praise, laud, glorify, extol, honor, bless, exalt, and acclaim the One who performed all these wonders for our ancestors and for us. He brought us from slavery to freedom, and from sorrow to joy, and from mourning to festivity, and from darkness to light, and from bondage to redemption.

Let us therefore sing a new song before him. Hallelujah!

(Put down the wineglass. To continue with the service, go to page 70.)

Passover is a story about Jews, but it is also a universal story about oppressed people yearning for freedom. This would be a good point in the service to make that connection and empha- size the relevance of the Seder for all faith traditions. You can ask your guests to relate a contemporary story that reminds them of Passover, or discuss a leader who resembles Moses, or say simply what freedom means to them. Rabbi Jill Jacobs of the Jewish Funds for Justice suggests asking guests to bring something that reminds them of the Passover story: a memento from their own family's immigration to America, for example, or a news story about a contemporary liberation struggle. One idea that we like: have guests read quotations from notable non-Jews that echo the Passover story and its message. Here are a few that are meaningful to us:

> To be free is not merely to cast off one's chains, but to live in a way that respects and enhances the freedom of others.
>
> —Nelson Mandela

> Change does not roll in on the wheels of inevitability, but comes through continuous struggle. And so we must straighten our backs and work for our freedom. A man can't ride you unless your back is bent.
>
> —Martin Luther King Jr.

> When I despair, I remember that all through history the way of truth and love has always won. There have been tyrants and murderers and for a time they seem invincible but in the end, they always fall—think of it, ALWAYS.
>
> —Mohandas K. Gandhi

> If the first woman God ever made was strong enough to turn the world upside down all alone, these women together ought to be able to turn it back, and get it right side up again! And now they is asking to do it, the men better let them.
>
> —Sojourner Truth

The older I get, the greater power I seem to have to help the world; I am like a snowball—the further I am rolled, the more I gain.

—Susan B. Anthony

Every time we liberate a woman, we liberate a man.

—Margaret Mead

There is a special place in hell for women who do not help other women.

—Madeleine Korbel Albright

The world has never yet seen a truly great and virtuous nation because in the degradation of woman the very fountains of life are poisoned at their source.

—Lucretia Mott

It is possible to become discouraged about the injustice we see everywhere. But God did not promise us that the world would be humane and just. He gives us the gift of life and allows us to choose the way we will use our limited time on earth. It is an awesome opportunity.

—Cesar Chavez

Freedom consists not in doing what we like, but in having the right to do what we ought.

—Pope John Paul II

Now that we are poor, we are free. No white man controls our footsteps. If we must die, we die defending our rights.

—Sitting Bull

You have heard that they were told, "Love your neighbor and hate your enemy." But what I tell you is this: Love your enemies and pray for your persecutors.

—Jesus Christ

God doesn't require us to succeed; He only requires that you try.

—Mother Teresa

Willingly no one chooses the yoke of slavery.

—Aeschylus

Our reliance is in the love of liberty which God has planted in our bosoms. Our defense is in the preservation of the spirit which prizes liberty as the heritage of all men, in all lands, everywhere.

—Abraham Lincoln

HALLEL: SONGS OF PRAISE

(We have everyone say this together.)

Hallelujah! Praise O ye servants of the Lord,
Praise the name of the Lord.
Praised be the name of the Lord,
Henceforth and forever more!
From the rising of the sun unto the going
   down thereof,
Praised be the name of the Lord,
Above the heavens is his glory.
Who is like the Lord our God,

That is enthroned on high,

That looks down low

Upon the heavens and the earth?

Who raises up the poor out of the dust

And lifts up the needy out of the dunghill.

That he may give him a seat among princes,

Among the princes of his people.

Who makes the barren woman to dwell in her
house,

As a joyful mother of children. Hallelujah!

When Israel came forth out of Egypt,

The house of Jacob from a people of strange
language,

Judah became his sanctuary,

Israel his dominion.

The sea saw it and fled;

The Jordan turned backward.

The mountains skipped like rams,

The hills like young sheep.

What ails thee, O sea, that thou flee?

Thou Jordan that thou turns backward?

Ye mountains that ye skip like rams?

Ye hills like young sheep?

Tremble thou earth, at the presence of the
Lord,

At the presence of the God of Jacob!

Who turned the rock into a pool of water,

The flint into a fountain of waters.

(Raise the cup of wine and say together.)

*Blessed be Thou, O Lord our God, Ruler of the
Universe, who has redeemed us and our ancestors
from Egypt and has enabled us to reach this
night where we eat unleavened bread and bitter
herbs. Thus, O Lord our God, and God of our
ancestors, thou enablest us to reach other holidays
and festivals [May they come to us in peace!],
rejoicing in Zion upbuilt and delighting in thy
service. And we will thank thee in new song for
our redemption and deliverance. Blessed be thou O
Lord who has redeemed Israel.*

בָּרוּךְ אַתָּה יהוה אֱלֹהֵינוּ מֶלֶךְ הָעוֹלָם בּוֹרֵה פְּרִי הַגָּפֶן.

Barukh atah Adonai eloheinu melekh ha-olam,
   borei p'ri ha-gafen.

Blessed be Thou, O Lord our God, Ruler of the
   Universe, who creates the fruit of the vine.

(Drink the second cup of wine.)

WASHING THE HANDS

(This is done a second time in preparation for dinner. The ritual derives from the edict that Orthodox Jews wash their hands and say a blessing each time they eat bread. As before, real hand washing with a big crowd is complicated. In our Seders only the leader has a washing bowl and performs the symbolic act for everyone. For others who want to participate, we suggest wetting fingertips in the little bowls of salt water used earlier in the service to dip parsley. They won't be used anymore for food.

בָּרוּךְ אַתָּה יהוה אֱלֹהֵנוּ מֶלֶךְ הָעוֹלָם אֲשֶׁר קִדְּשָׁנוּ בְּמִצְוֹתָיו וְצִוָּנוּ עַל־נְטִילַת יָדָיִם.

Barukh atah Adonai eloheinu melekh ha-olam,
Asher kid'shanu be-mitzvotav ve-tzivanu al n'tilat
   y'dayim.

Blessed be Thou, O Lord our God, Ruler of
   the Universe, who has sanctified us with thy
   commandments and bidden us wash our hands.

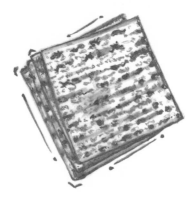

BLESSING THE MATZO

(The leader takes the two whole matzos, and the
broken middle one, and passes them around so
that each guest receives a piece. Or guests can
use the matzo set at their places. The blessings
are familiar and can be said in both English and
Hebrew.)

בָּרוּךְ אַתָּה יהוה אֱלֹהֵנוּ מֶלֶךְ הָעוֹלָם הַמּוֹצִיא לֶחֶם מִן הָאָרֶץ.

*Barukh atah Aдonai eloheinu melekh ha-olam, ha-
motzi lekhem min ha-aretz.*

Blessed be thou, O Lord our God, Ruler of the Universe, who brings forth bread from the earth.

בָּרוּךְ אַתָּה יהוה אֱלֹהֵנוּ מֶלֶךְ הָעוֹלָם אֲשֶׁר קִדְּשָׁנוּ בְּמִצְוֹתָיו וְצִוָּנוּ עַל־אֲכִילַת מַצָּה.

Barukh atah Adonai eloheinu melekh ha-olam, asher kid'shanu be-mitzvotav ve-tzivanu al akhilat matzah.

Blessed be thou, O Lord our God, Ruler of the Universe, who has sanctified us with thy commandments and bidden us to eat unleavened bread.

(Everyone takes a bite of matzo.)

EAT THE BITTER HERBS

(Take the *maror*, the bitter herbs [horseradish] and dip them into the *haroset*. Say together:)

May the sweet *haroset* that we eat with these bitter herbs symbolize for us the hope of freedom that enabled our ancestors to withstand the bitterness of their slavery.

(Then say the following blessing:)

Barukh atah Adonai eloeim melekh ha-olam, asher kid'shanu be-mitzvotav ve-tzivanu al akhilat maror.

בָּרוּךְ אַתָּה יהוה אֱלֹהֵנוּ מֶלֶךְ הָעוֹלָם אֲשֶׁר קִדְּשָׁנוּ בְּמִצְוֹתָיו וְצִוָּנוּ עַל־אֲכִילַת מָרוֹר.

Blessed be Thou, O Lord our God, Ruler of the Universe who has sanctified us with thy commandments and bidden us to eat bitter herbs.

HILLEL SANDWICH

(Put the bitter herbs and the *haroset* between two pieces of matzo to create the "Hillel sandwich." Then say the following:)

Thus did the great Hillel when the Temple in Jerusalem was still standing: he would place together some of the Paschal Lamb and some *maror* with matzo and eat them as one to fulfill the biblical command: "Together with unleavened bread and bitter herbs shall they eat the Paschal Lamb."

Rabbi Hillel was a revered Jewish sage born in the first century BCE. He originally included slivers of Paschal Lamb in his "sandwich" but that practice ended after the Temple in Jerusalem was destroyed and animal sacrifice was no longer practiced. Because Hillel was also known as a gifted teacher, his name lives on today in the foundations that organize and sponsor Jewish life on more than 500 U.S. college campuses.

DINNER

(See the end of the book for suggested recipes.)

(The leader can direct the children to look for the *afikomen* either during or after dinner. If the kids finish eating before the adults, which is likely, the hunt is a good way to keep them occupied while you savor your dessert. It's customary to have a small present for the finder of the *afikomen*. The finder brings the *afikomen* to the leader, who is supposed to share it among the guests, but that's a little hard with a big crowd. Even so, everyone should have a last bite of matzo.)

THE GRACE AFTER THE MEAL

(Say together:)

Blessed be God of whose bounty we have eaten and by whose goodness we live. May God bless this home, the people at this table, and all of our loved ones who are not here with us tonight. May God bring peace to all homes, all nations, and all faith traditions.

THE THIRD CUP OF WINE: REDEMPTION

(Fill the third cup of wine. Say the following together:)

We now fill our cups for the third time, in thanksgiving for the festive meal we have just eaten.

Blessed be Thou, O Lord our God, Ruler of the Universe, who sustains all humanity in thy goodness. Thy mercy endureth forever. Through thy great kindness we have never been in want of food. May we never suffer for want of food. Praised

be thou, O Lord, who provides for all the creatures
Thou hast created.

בָּרוּךְ אַתָּה יהוה אֱלֹהֵינוּ מֶלֶךְ הָעוֹלָם בּוֹרֵא פְּרִי הַגָּפֶן.

Barukh atah Adonai eloheinu melekh ha-olam,
borei p'ri ha-gafen.

Blessed be Thou, O Lord our God, Ruler of the
Universe, who creates the fruit of the vine.

(Drink the third cup and then the leader fills
Elijah's cup. In some traditions, and with smaller
crowds, everyone at the table can contribute a bit
to Elijah's cup, a sign that all share the hope for a
better future that the prophet represents.)

THE CUP OF ELIJAH

(The leader asks for the door to be opened, usually by a child, who is instructed to see if Elijah has arrived. The cup is raised while everyone says:)

This cup of wine is called Elijah's cup. The prophet Elijah, according the Jewish tradition, will herald the Messiah. So let us sing together the song of Elijah:

Elijah the Prophet, Elijah the Tishbite,
Elijah, Elijah, Elijah the Gileadite,
Soon may he come, bringing with him Messiah.

According to legend Elijah lived in a cave on Mount Carmel in the ninth century BCE, near the present-day city of Haifa. Because of his fierce defense of God in the face of pagan practices, he became known as the "guardian angel" of the Hebrew people. In the book of Kings it is written that Elijah never really died but ascended to heaven in a flaming chariot. In the book of Malachi God says: "Look, I shall send you the prophet Elijah before the great and terrible day of the Lord comes. He will reconcile parents to children and children to parents, lest I come and put the land under a ban to destroy it." Then there's his name. "Tishbite" can mean "stranger" or "dweller," so one reading of the verse means "Elijah, a stranger [or dweller] from Gilead." Others say Tishbe was a place in Gilead, so "Tishbite" refers to his hometown. In any case it's a charming ritual that the children especially enjoy.

The Hebrew song "Eliyahu ha-Navi" expresses the same feeling. We can say it together, and those of you who know the tune can then sing it.

Eliyahu ha-Navi
Eliyahu ha-Tishbi
Eliyahu, Eliyahu, Eliyahu ha-Giladi.

Bi-m'herah be-yameinu yavo eleinu
Im mashiah ben David,
Im mashiah ben David.

HALLEL: SONGS OF PRAISE

(Fill the fourth cup of wine. We say the following prayer together:)

We fill our cups for the fourth time before singing our songs of praise.

Praise the Lord all ye nations;
Laud him all ye peoples!
For his loving kindness is mighty over us,
And the truth of the Lord endureth forever.
Hallelujah!

Give thanks unto the Eternal, for He is good,
For His mercy endureth forever.
Let Israel now say,
That His mercy endureth forever.
Let the house of Aaron now say,
That His mercy endureth forever.
Let those who fear the Eternal now say,
That His mercy endureth forever.

Give thanks unto the Eternal, for He is gracious,
For His mercy endureth forever.
Give thanks unto the God of Gods,
For His mercy endureth forever.
Give thanks to the Lord of Lords,
For His mercy endureth forever.
Unto Him who alone performs wondrous deeds,
For His mercy endureth forever.
Unto Him who made the heavens in wisdom,
For His mercy endureth forever.
Who did expand the earth above the waters,
For His mercy endureth forever.

Who made great lights,

For His mercy endureth forever.

The sun to rule by day,

For His mercy endureth forever.

The moon and stars to rule by night,

For His mercy endureth forever.

Who smote the Egyptians and their firstborn,

For His mercy endureth forever.

And brought out Israel from among them,

For His mercy endureth forever.

With a strong hand and outstretched arm,

For His mercy endureth forever.

Who divided the Red Sea into two,

For His mercy endureth forever.

And caused Israel to pass through the midst of it,

For His mercy endureth forever.

And overthrew Pharaoh and his hosts in the Red
      Sea,

For His mercy endureth forever.

To Him who guided His people through the
      wilderness,

For His mercy endureth forever.

Who smote great kings,

For His mercy endureth forever.

And slew mighty kings,

For His mercy endureth forever.

Sihon, king of the Amorites,

For His mercy endureth forever.

And Og, king of Bashan,

For His mercy endureth forever.

And gave their land as an inheritance,

For His mercy endureth forever.

As an inheritance to Israel, his servant,

For His mercy endureth forever.

Who remembered us in our humiliation,

For His mercy endureth forever.

And redeemed us from our oppressors,

For His mercy endureth forever.

Who gives food unto all flesh,

For His mercy endureth forever.

O give thanks unto the God of heaven,

For His mercy endureth forever.

SINGING

(This part is optional, but we have some
enthusiastic singers among our regular guests, and
this is a joyful way to end the Seder. "Had Gadya"
is the most traditional song but most non-Jews
are not familiar with it, so spirituals and folk
songs are probably a better bet. Lyrics to some
of the songs that make our annual hit parade are
included at the end of the Haggadah.)

THE FOURTH CUP OF WINE: RESTORATION

WE ARE ABOUT TO DRINK THE FOURTH CUP OF WINE.

בָּרוּךְ אַתָּה יהוה אֱלֹ הֵנוּ מֶלֶךְ הָעוֹלָם בּוֹרֵה פְּרִי הַגָּפֶן.

Barukh atah Adonai eloheinu melekh ha-olam,
borei p'ri ha-gafen.

Blessed be Thou, O Lord our God, Ruler of the
Universe, who creates the fruit of the vine.

(Drink the fourth cup. Then we say the final
portion in unison:)

Our Seder has come to an end. We have fulfilled all of its commandments—we have eaten the matzo, we have told the story of the Exodus, we have drunk our four cups of wine, we have partaken of bitter herbs, and we have sung our songs of praise unto the Lord. We have remembered that Israel's struggle for liberation from bondage echoes through the centuries, calling us to fight tyranny today—in all forms and in all places.

We have celebrated in freedom and friendship. May we do so again next year, all of us together, with joy and in peace.

AFTERWORD

ﾟ⤜ﾟ

Share the Seder

As an interfaith couple we have always tried to em-
phasize our shared values, not our differences. We
have tried to educate, not convert, each other. And
we cherish the moments that transcend doctrinal
disagreement and transmit a single spiritual message.
At the Western Wall in Jerusalem, Judaism's holiest
site, we placed prayers in the craggy stones, honoring
our ancestors. And on a sun-splashed morning outside of Rome, we watched Pope John Paul II, dressed
in simple white vestments, kneel a few feet away in
silent devotion. But no season better symbolizes our
common heritage than this one. Spring. The season
of rebirth and renewal, of freedom and fertility, of

the Seder and the Last Supper. Our Haggadah tells a Jewish story, but it also tells a human story, a story that all faith traditions can understand and embrace. In 1988, at the Vatican's urging, the United States Conference of Catholic Bishops instructed priests to recognize in their homilies "the deep spiritual bond between Judaism and Christianity." And while that bond is most visible during Passover and Easter, said the bishops, it should inform Catholic teaching throughout the year: "We must . . . accept our responsibility to prepare the world for the coming of the Messiah by working together for social justice, respect for the rights of persons and nations, and for social and international reconciliation. To this we are driven, Jews and Christians, by the command to love our neighbor, by a common hope for the kingdom of God, and by the great heritage of the prophets." Our "common hope" is that this Haggadah will inspire you to celebrate your own "great heritage"—as a family and a community. Bring a blessing. Tell the story. Share the Seder.

SEDER SONGS

✦

Ha∂ Ga∂ya

Had gadya
Had gadya
My father bought for two zuzim
Had gadya
Had gadya

Then came the cat
And ate the kid
My father bought for two zuzim
REFRAIN

Then came the dog
And bit the cat
That ate the kid
My father bought for two zuzim

"Had Gadya" is the most traditional of Seder songs. It has a very complicated history and an even more complicated meaning. Here's what Jewish Heritage Online Magazine says: "Most scholars agree that 'Had Gadya' was borrowed from a late medieval German folk song ('Der Herr der schickt den Jokel aus'), which, in turn, is based on an old French nursery song. The song, translated into the various vernaculars used by Jews and set to local tunes, makes its first appearance as a Passover song in a Haggadah printed in Prague in 1590. It was never part of the Sephardi [Spanish] and the Yemenite rituals." As for its meaning, Jewish Heritage writes: "Despite its likely origin, 'Had Gadya' has been vested by Jewish commentators with allegorical meaning. According to one popular interpretation, the kid symbolizes the oppressed Jewish people, which was bought by the father (God) for two coins (Moses and Aaron). The subsequent players in the ballad represent the nations who persecuted the Jewish people over the centuries: the devouring cat represents Assyria; the dog, Babylon; the stick represents Persia; the fire, Macedonia; the water is Rome; the ox, the Saracens; the *shohet* (ritual slaughterer), the Crusaders; and the Angel of Death, the Turks, who subsequently ruled Palestine. The end of the song expresses the hope for messianic redemption: God destroys the foreign rulers of the Holy Land and vindicates Israel as 'the only kid.' " If you're not familiar with the song or the tune, there are many free recordings available online that can get you up to speed.

REFRAIN

Then came the stick
And beat the dog
That bit the cat
That ate the kid
My father bought for two zuzim
REFRAIN

Then came the fire
That burned the stick
That beat the dog
That bit the cat
That ate the kid
My father bought for two zuzim
REFRAIN

Then came the water
That quenched the fire
That burned the stick
That beat the dog
That bit the cat
That ate the kid
My father bought for two zuzim

REFRAIN

Then came the ox
That drank the water
That quenched the fire
That burned the stick
That beat the dog
That bit the cat
That ate the kid
My father bought for two zuzim

REFRAIN

Then came the butcher
That slew the ox
That drank the water
That quenched the fire
That burned the stick
That beat the dog
That bit the cat
That ate the kid
My father bought for two zuzim

REFRAIN

Then came the Angel of Death
And killed the butcher
That slew the ox
That drank the water
That quenched the fire
That burned the stick
That beat the dog
That bit the cat
That ate the kid
My father bought for two zuzim

REFRAIN

Then came the Holy One
Blessed be He
And destroyed the Angel of Death
That killed the butcher
That slew the ox
That drank the water
That quenched the fire
That burned the stick
That beat the dog

That bit the cat
That ate the kid
My father bought for two zuzim
REFRAIN

*African American spirituals, with the theme of free-
dom running through them, make perfect Passover
songs. Most people already know the words to old favorites like "Michael, Row Your Boat Ashore." But
the most appropriate Seder song of all is the spiritual
that actually tells the story of the Exodus: "Go Down,
Moses."*

❧

Go Down, Moses

When Israel was in Egypt's land,
Let My people go!
Oppressed so hard they could not stand,
Let My people go!

Go down, Moses,
Way down in Egypt's land;
Tell old Pharaoh
To let My people go!

No more shall they in bondage toil,
Let My people go!
Let them come out with Egypt's spoil,
Let My people go!

You need not always weep and mourn,
Let My people go!
And wear these slav'ry chains forlorn,
Let My people go!

Your foes shall not before you stand,
Let My people go!
And you'll possess fair Canaan's land,
Let My people go!

Rise and Shine

This song really has nothing to do with Passover except that it's biblical. But when she was a little girl, our friend Taylor Latham contributed it to the repertoire, and it's been part of our Seder ever since, referred to always as "Taylor's Song."

REFRAIN:

Rise and shine

And give God the glory, glory

Rise and shine

And give God the glory, glory

Rise and shine

And give God the glory, glory

Children of the Lord

The Lord said to Noah:

There's gonna be a floody, floody

The Lord said to Noah:

There's gonna be a floody, floody

Get those children out of the muddy, muddy

Children of the Lord

So Noah
He built him, he built him an arky, arky
Noah
He built him, he built him an arky, arky
Built it out of gopher barky, barky
Children of the Lord

The animals, the animals,
They came in by twosie, twosies
The animals, the animals,
They came in by twosie, twosies
Elephants and kangaroosie, roosies
Children of the Lord

It rained and poured
For forty daysie, daysies
It rained and poured
For forty daysie, daysies
Nearly drove those animals
    crazy, crazies, crazies
Children of the Lord

The sun came out and
dried up the landy, landy
The sun came out and
dried up the landy, landy
Everything was fine and dandy, dandy
Children of the Lord

REFRAIN

The animals they came off
They came off by three-sies, three-sies
Animals they came off
They came off by three-sies, three-sies
Grizzly bears and chimpanzee-sies, zee-sies
Children of the Lord

REFRAIN

That is the end of,
The end of my story, story
That is the end of,
The end of my story, story
Everything is hunky dory, dory
Children of the Lord

REFRAIN

❦

We Shall Overcome

We shall overcome, we shall overcome,
We shall overcome someday,
Oh, deep in my heart I do believe
We shall overcome someday.

We'll walk hand in hand, we'll walk
    hand in hand,
We'll walk hand in hand someday,
Oh, deep in my heart I do believe
We shall overcome someday.

We are not afraid, we are not afraid.
We are not afraid today,
Oh, deep in my heart I do believe
We shall overcome someday.

We shall stand together, we shall stand together,
We shall stand together—now,
Oh, deep in my heart I do believe
We shall overcome someday.

The truth will make us free, the truth will make us
   free,
The truth will make us free someday,
Oh, deep in my heart I do believe
We shall overcome someday.

The Lord will see us through, the Lord will see us
   through,
The Lord will see us through someday,
Oh, deep in my heart I do believe
We shall overcome someday.

We shall be like Him, we shall be like Him,
We shall be like Him someday,
Oh, deep in my heart I do believe
We shall overcome someday.

We shall live in peace, we shall live in peace,
We shall live in peace someday,
Oh, deep in my heart I do believe
We shall overcome someday.

The whole wide world around, the whole wide
   world around,

The whole wide world around someday,
Oh, deep in my heart I do believe
We shall overcome someday.

We shall overcome, we shall overcome.
We shall overcome someday,
Oh, deep in my heart I do believe
We shall overcome someday.

COKIE'S RECIPES

⊶⊷

First a note on the term "kosher for Passover": many items in the grocery stores bear that label, and it means that a rabbi has officially given the product a seal of approval. But that's where any agreement ends. Sephardic Jews, those who hail from the shores of the Mediterranean, have very different views of what's acceptable at Passover from the Ashkenazic, or European, Jews. The Ashkenazim abstain from lamb at Passover as a way to commemorate the destruction of the Temple of Jerusalem in 70 CE. With no Temple, there was no sacrifice of the Paschal Lamb, so the European Jews developed the tradition of serving some other meat or fish at their Seders, and the Orthodox use no roasted meat. That's not true of Sephardic Jews, who traditionally do serve lamb. Then there's the question of what constitutes leavening, or *hametz*. In addition to the prohibition against all bread products and anything (other than matzo) from flour, wheat, barley, rye, oats, and spelt (an ancient form of wheat), Ashkenazim also forbid rice, dried beans, peas, and lentils. However, the Sephardim don't share those restrictions. Since I like Middle Eastern food a lot better than eastern European or German food, the Sephardic tradition is the one I go with, especially since I think it's more appropriate for a feast that began in Egypt. When some of our friends of European Jewish descent look askance at some of my menu choices, I'm glad to have the Sephardic rabbis' rulings to back me up. There are also arguments about what alcoholic beverages are kosher for Passover. Clearly, nothing made from grain would be. If you care, you can buy kosher for Passover liquors and liqueurs. If your local liquor store doesn't have them, look online at Web sites such as kosherwine.com. That site also has many good-looking kosher wines, and our editor insists that she serves an "amazing" kosher version of Sancerre. But I've never tried them.

Hors d'Oeuvres

GEFILTE FISH

Buy it in jars at the grocery store (or you can order it from Amazon.com). One jar is usually sufficient for however many people you have—there will still be some left over. Take it out of the yucky gelatinous broth and cut it into slices. Put it on a plate or tray with some toothpicks and put some horseradish in a bowl for those who want to add it to the fish. We use red horseradish for this because the gefilte fish is grayish white.

You can, of course, make your own gefilte fish. It's ground fish—usually a combination of carp, whitefish, and pike—with filler. For Passover the filler would be matzo meal. My friend Joan Nathan has several recipes using different kinds of fish in her very smart cookbook *Jewish Cooking in America*. But they all look long and complicated, so I haven't tried them. (Recently I found a note to myself stuck in Joan's book: "Don't forget zucchini with raisins and pine nuts for Passover." Apparently one year I tucked the piece of paper with the makings of that dish in the back cover. Recipe later.)

CHOPPED CHICKEN LIVERS

This recipe is in Joan's book. She got it from one of Washington's most beloved characters—Hyman Bookbinder, called Bookie, the longtime lobbyist for the American Jewish Committee. Once Joan and Bookie were making the chopped liver for Joan's TV show and she arranged for me to show up as a surprise to add the ingredient that I said this recipe lacked: Tabasco.

4 large eggs
3 to 4 tablespoons vegetable oil
3 medium onions, diced
¼ green pepper, diced (optional)
1 pound fresh chicken livers
Salt and pepper to taste
1 tablespoon chicken fat (optional)

Boil the eggs, heat the oil, and sauté the onions and green pepper over a high heat for about 5 minutes. Add the chicken livers and cook until firm, about 5 minutes. Don't overcook. Chop the mixture together with sliced eggs (you can use a food processor, but don't puree the mix). Add salt and pepper. Add chicken fat if you want. (I also add Tabasco, and usually some spicy mustard and maybe a little cognac.)

Crudité

Carrots, and whatever other raw vegetables you think the children might eat, since they are likely to get hungry before dinner, served with hummus. There are so many good types of store-bought hummus now available that we've abandoned our homemade recipe.

EGGPLANT SALAD

This recipe is taken from Barbara Kafka's *Microwave Gourmet*. Ovens newer than the 700-watt microwave in which this recipe was tested may give a different result. Try using 70 percent of the power for the newest ovens.

> *1 large eggplant, pricked several times with a fork*
> *1 small onion, peeled and chopped, about ½ cup*
> *¼ cup chopped parsley*
> *1 clove garlic, smashed, peeled, and minced*
> *1 teaspoon kosher salt*
> *¼ teaspoon freshly ground pepper*
> *2 tablespoons olive oil*
> *2 tablespoons fresh lemon juice*

Put eggplant on top of a few paper towels and cook in the microwave on high for 12 minutes. Remove from oven and let cool. Cut it in half lengthwise and scoop out flesh. Put the flesh in a food processor and add onions, parsley, garlic, salt, and pepper and process until coarsely chopped. Put in serving bowl and

stir in oil and lemon juice. Serve at room temperature with matzo.

SALMON SPREAD

1 one-pound can of salmon
3 tablespoons mayonnaise
1½ tablespoons tarragon vinegar
1 teaspoon capers
1 tablespoon minced chives
1 or 2 big drops of Tabasco

Remove skin and bones from the salmon. Put everything in the food processor and run it until you have
a smooth pate. Put it in a serving bowl and stir in
some more capers if you like. Serve with matzo.

Recipes for Dinner

When we got married, Nan Robertson, the Pulitzer
Prize–winning *New York Times* reporter, gave us

Craig Claiborne's *The New York Times Cookbook* as a wedding present, saying that we would find it invaluable. As usual, she was right. The covers are long gone, along with much of the index and the first twenty pages of the book, but the recipes I've used year in and year out for Passover are still intact. The ones below come from there, somewhat adapted for Passover, unless otherwise noted.

AVGOLEMONO (EGG-LEMON) SOUP

2 quarts strong chicken broth
½ cup raw rice
4 eggs
Juice of 2 lemons

Serves 6 to 8

Boil broth and add rice, cook till rice is tender, about 20 minutes. Remove from heat. Just before service, beat eggs with electric beater until light and frothy. Slowly beat in lemon juice and dilute mixture with 2 cups of hot soup, beating constantly until well mixed. Add the diluted egg-lemon mixture to the rest of the soup, beating constantly (preferably with electric hand beater). Bring almost to boiling point but don't boil because soup will curdle. Serve immediately. (Now you see why we don't serve it anymore, but it's really delicious and so springlike.)

LEG OF LAMB,
MIDDLE EASTERN STYLE

You can see that as a twenty-five-year-old cooking for my first Seder, I was pretty literal when it came to choosing something that looked appropriate for Passover.

5-pound leg of lamb
Salt and pepper to taste
1 bunch scallions, chopped (tops and bottoms)
8 stalks fresh mint, chopped
1 cup beef stock

Serves 6 to 8

Preheat oven to 450°F, rub meat with salt and pepper. Put meat on rack if you have one and roast for about 15 minutes or until brown. Reduce heat to 325°F and continue roasting about 10 more minutes. Cover with scallions and mint, add stock to pan. Cook until desired degree of doneness, probably about 15 more minutes for rare (140°F on meat thermometer), basting with pan juices. (Steve and I like our lamb rare, some of our guests would like it better done—Claiborne says to cook until 175°F on thermometer. I've personally never used a meat thermometer, so you need to stop cooking the meat at the doneness you like.) Serve with the scallions and mint. Serves 6 to 8, depending on how many meat-eaters there are in your gang and how much bone is in the lamb. My rule of thumb is about 8 ounces per adult. You need to have the meat done in time to cut out the bone and put it on the Seder plate.

We serve it with mint jelly and Crosse & Blackwell mint sauce because our troops demand them, but they're not exactly in keeping with the Middle Eastern theme.

DRIED BEAN SALAD

2 cups canned white Navy beans (you can start from scratch and cook the beans, but it's a lot more work and they don't taste as good for salad)

¼ cup olive oil

Juice of 1 lemon

Salt and pepper to taste

Chopped parsley, dill, and mint (or you can skip the mint, since the lamb has it)

4 scallions, chopped

1 hard-cooked egg (optional, but it's really good)

1 tomato (optional, and we skip it partly because there are tomatoes in other dishes)

Serves 6

Drain beans. Put oil, lemon juice, salt and pepper in bowl and blend thoroughly. Add beans, mix well, scatter chopped herbs and scallions over beans, mix carefully. Add egg quarters (and tomatoes).

We serve those two dishes every Passover. And though we don't cater to everyone's dietary demands, we do have one friend who has had heart trouble and doesn't eat red meat. So we always sauté a piece of fish for him and do a little extra for other non-meat-eaters.

We do vary the vegetables from year to year. Here are some we have prepared:

ZUCCHINI IN A SKILLET

2 tablespoons oil
1 medium onion slice
1 cup chopped tomatoes, canned or fresh
¾ teaspoon salt
Pepper to taste
½ bay leaf
3 medium zucchini, cut in 1-inch pieces

Serves 4

Heat the oil, add onions, and sauté until transparent. Add tomatoes, salt, pepper, and bay leaf, and simmer

5 minutes. Add zucchini, cover, and simmer until tender, about 8 to 10 minutes. Remove bay leaf.

CREOLE OKRA

We love okra, and it certainly grows in Egypt, but it can be a hard sell to a crowd. I generally just make up the recipe as I go along, but here is Claiborne's version.

2 tablespoons oil
¼ cup minced onion
3 tablespoons minced green pepper
1½ cups sliced okra (you can buy it frozen already sliced; Trappey's canned okra is also good)
2 cups canned or fresh tomatoes, peeled (or not! I never peel tomatoes) and chopped
Pinch of basil
Salt and pepper to taste
Healthy dash of Tabasco

Serves 4

Heat oil, cook onion and green pepper until soft, add okra, and sauté over medium heat about 5 minutes, stirring. Lower heat, add rest of ingredients and simmer, covered, about 20 minutes. Add water if it starts to scorch.

ZUCCHINI WITH RAISINS AND PINE NUTS

This is the one tucked into the back of Joan Nathan's cookbook. It's off the *Epicurious* Web site, www .epicurious.com. It's from the book *Crossroads Cooking,* by Elizabeth Rozin.

> 2 to 3 tablespoons olive oil
> 3 large cloves garlic
> 4 small to medium zucchini, trimmed and cut
>   about ½ inch thick
> 2 medium tomatoes, coarsely chopped
> 1 teaspoon anchovy paste
> 2 tablespoons golden raisins
> 1 tablespoon red wine vinegar
> Black pepper to taste
> 1 tablespoon pine nuts, lightly toasted

Serves 4 to 6

Heat oil and sauté garlic over moderate heat, stirring until garlic begins to turn golden. Don't brown it. Add zucchini and sauté for a few minutes, stirring. Add everything else except pepper and pine nuts and mix well. Cook about 10 to 12 minutes, stirring occasionally. Add pepper and nuts. Serve at room temperature.

As you can see, there's a theme to these vegetable recipes. They all have a mix of vegetables and all have tomatoes because the plates need the color with the meat and beans. Of course you can always just roast a bunch of vegetables and some potatoes with the meat. Nothing's simpler and everyone loves them.

For a dish more unique to Passover, try this one from Joan Nathan.

EGGPLANT AND GREEN PEPPER KUGEL (CASSEROLE)

1 large eggplant (about 2 pounds)
1 onion, diced

1 green pepper, diced
2 tablespoons pine nuts
¼ cup olive oil
2 tablespoons chopped fresh basil
Salt and pepper to taste
2 large eggs, lightly beaten
1 matzo, crumbled
2 tablespoons butter or margarine

Serves 6 to 8

Preheat oven to 350°F. Peel eggplant and dice into 2-inch cubes. Cook in simmering salted water to cover until tender, about 20 minutes. Drain and mash (I use a food processor). Sauté onion, pepper, and pine nuts in olive oil over medium heat until vegetables are tender but not crisp. Combine with basil, salt, and pepper. Mix it all together with the eggplant and eggs. Add the matzo and continue to mix. Put the whole mixture in a greased casserole. Dot with butter or margarine. Cook 35 minutes or until golden brown on top and crusty on the sides.

When I do that dish I also roast a lot of cherry tomatoes for some color on the plates.

I have always enjoyed the bean salad with lamb, but if you don't like beans, there are many ways to give rice dishes a Middle Eastern flavor:

Here are two suggestions: Make the rice the way you would for a pilaf. So, first chop 1 large onion. Heat a few tablespoons of olive oil—2 to 3—and sauté the chopped onion until soft. Then stir in a cup of long-grain rice (preferably Uncle Ben's Original— the converted rice is almost foolproof), and coat the grains with the oil. Add 1½ cups of chicken broth and bring to a boil. (I know most people add more liquid, but this is the way my mother taught me, and I'm sticking to it.) Reduce the heat and cover the pot. The rice should be done in about 20 to 25 minutes. Toast some pine nuts (I toast them in the microwave for about a minute), then stir those in, along with some raisins, dill, and mint—as you prefer—and add salt and pepper to taste. My rule of thumb on rice is that, as a side dish, 1 cup serves about 4 people.

Obviously you wouldn't make this dish if you had chosen the zucchini with raisins and pine nuts.

In Greece we regularly had the traditional *spanakorizo*, or spinach rice, with lamb dishes. And now that you can buy those bags of prewashed spinach, the dish is really easy to make. Chop 2 to 3 medium onions. Heat some olive oil—about ½ cup—and sauté the onions until soft. Add 2 to 3 bags of prewashed spinach until it wilts—just a few minutes. Then add either a can of tomato sauce or 1 tablespoon of tomato paste diluted with 1 cup of water, and another cup of liquid, either water or broth, and bring to a boil. Season with some parsley, dill, salt, and pepper, all to taste and your preference. Sprinkle about ½ cup of rice on top, reduce the heat, and cover the pot. Add more liquid if it seems necessary. It should be done in about 25 minutes. This dish is good at room temperature, which is great, because it means you can have it ready ahead of time and be able to serve it quickly when the Seder takes a hiatus.

❦

Dessert

MACAROONS

This is the traditional Passover dessert. Our guests usually bring them or we buy them. Joan Nathan has a couple of interesting recipes for pistachio or pecan macaroons, but we haven't tried them. Another of Joan's dessert recipes for Passover, however, is a favorite:

ABSOLUTELY EASY AND ABSOLUTELY DELICIOUS CHOCOLATE TORTE

1 stick unsalted butter or margarine
8 ounces bittersweet chocolate
5 large eggs, separated
¾ cup sugar
1 cup ground almonds

Serves 8 to 10

Preheat oven to 375°F. Melt butter or margarine with the chocolate in top of a double boiler (microwave works fine). Cool. Beat egg yolks with sugar until pale yellow. Mix cooled butter or margarine and chocolate with sugar and yolks. Add nuts. Beat egg whites until stiff but not dry. Fold into chocolate mixture. Place pan of water in bottom of oven. Line bottom and side of greased 9-inch springform pan with aluminum foil and pour in filling. Bake 45 to 50 minutes. Remove from oven and let sit a few minutes. Unmold and carefully peel off foil and place upside down on cake plate. Sprinkle with sugar. Confectioners' is best but not kosher for Passover. Joan suggests grinding granulated sugar in food processor and using that.

We serve the torte and macaroons with our old standby, Craig Claiborne's Cardinal Strawberries:

CARDINAL STRAWBERRIES

¼ cup raspberry jam

2 tablespoons sugar

¼ cup water

1 tablespoon kirsch (or any other fruit-based sweet liqueur)

¼ cup slivered almonds

1 quart fresh strawberries

Serves 4

Combine jam, sugar, and water in saucepan and simmer about 2 minutes. Add liqueur and chill. Sprinkle almonds over sliced strawberries. Serve with the sauce.

As you see, there's nothing complicated here. In my case, it's the amount of food that causes the effort, not the difficulty of the dish. But they all taste good and will allow you to enjoy your own Seder. So do.

SOURCES AND WEB SITES

∽∾

The Internet makes shopping and preparing for Passover much easier. We've used the Source For Everything Jewish for many things over many years and always found it reliable. To order the catalog, call 800-426-2567. The Web site is www.jewishsource .com. Here is a list of additional links and Web sites we've discovered in writing this Haggadah.

Make Your Own Seder Plate Kits
http://www.jewishstore.com/Judaica/Products
.asp?ProdID=RL-PLATEK

Ten Plagues Masks
http://www.judaicaplace.com/rl_ppmask/judaica/
item.html

Ten Plagues Finger Puppets
http://www.jewishstore.com/Judaica/Products
.asp?ProdID=RL-TYPupTen

Ten Plagues in a Box and Other Passover Gifts
http://chai kids.com/site/776828/page/324480

Ten Plagues Place Mat Kits
http://www.grandparents.com/gp/content/
activitiesandevents/everyday-activities/article/
passover-crafts.html

Instructions for Acting Out the Ten Plagues As a Skit
http://www.aish.com/h/pes/f/48969191.html

A Lively Piano Version of "Dayenu"
http://www.theholidayspot.com/passover/music/

Sheet Music for "Dayenu" and Other Holiday Songs
http://www.musicnotes.com/sheetmusic/mtdVPE
.asp?ppn=MN0016421

A folk rock version of "Had Gadya" by Jeff Klepper on guitar and vocals is available on You Tube: http://il.youtube.com/watch?v=kWbFcwicwUo&a=GxdCwVVULXedyYUNr3s5Jp4J3dBUf–8F&playnext=1

Sheet Music for "Had Gadya"
http://www.musicnotes.com/sheetmusic/mtdVPE.asp?ppn=MN0028195

Kosher Wines and Liquors
http://www.kosherwine.com/

A Wide Variety of Products and Information, from a Passover Countdown Clock and Afikomen T-Shirts to Gift Baskets and Jokes
http://www.kosher4passover.com/

ACKNOWLEDGMENTS

This project started with a suggestion from Carolyn Starman Hessel, the able and enthusiastic director of the Jewish Book Council, who has always been a strong supporter of our work. We're deeply grateful. As always, we received invaluable help from our dear friend and editor, Claire Wachtel. This is the seventh volume she's shepherded into print for us, and this time she provided the Hebrew along with her usual menu of encouragement and wisdom. Many thanks to assistant editor Elizabeth Perrella; Leah Carlson-Stanisic; our publicist, Dee Dee DeBartlo; and at Harper Books, publisher Jonathan Burnham and associate publisher Kathy Schneider. The president of HarperCollins, Michael Morrison, has been a great supporter as well. The illustrator, Kristina Applegate-Lutes, has been very patient as we asked for new renditions of many of her delightful drawings. Our lawyer and friend, Bob Barnett, always gives us great guidance and many laughs. We could not put on our Seders without the invaluable help of a dedicated staff, headed by Pilar Hernandez, during the early days and now by Manuel Rouco. They show up and bail us out year after year. Kim Roellig has been keeping our lives straight for a long time. Special thanks to Steve's parents, Will and Dorothy Roberts, who were kind enough to hold our first Seder, at Cokie's request, and then traveled to be with us at many Passovers after we started our own rituals. Will died in 1997 and Dorothy died just as we were completing this book. She was enthusiastic about the project but always a little surprised—and very grateful—that her Catholic daughter-in-law had brought this Jewish ritual back to the Roberts family.